Silver Bullets

A TOC Workbook for Problem Solving

SHANE AYERS

Copyright © 2019 Shane Ayers

All rights reserved

ISBN: 9781799141334

This book is dedicated to my heroes, Feynman, Gottman and Goldratt. Better living through science today, tomorrow and forever.

Contents

Introduction 1
Section 1: Inner Dilemma 3
    Inner Dilemma Solution Steps: 3
    Inner Dilemma Worksheet 6
Section 2: Day-to-Day Conflicts 13
    Day-to-Day Conflict Solution Steps 13
    Day-to-Day Conflict Worksheet 16
Section 3: Firefighting Situations 23
    Firefighting Situation Solution Steps 23
    Firefighting Situation Worksheet 26
Section 4: Undesirable Effects 37
    Undesirable Effects Solution Steps 37
    Undesirable Effects Worksheet 41
Section 5: Three-Cloud Approach 48
    Three-Cloud Approach Solution Steps 48
    Three-Cloud Approach Worksheet 56
Appendix: Worksheets 81
    Inner Dilemma Worksheet 2 82
    Inner Dilemma Worksheet 3 89
    Inner Dilemma Worksheet 4 96
    Inner Dilemma Worksheet 5 103
    Day-to-Day Conflict Worksheet 2 110
    Day-to-Day Conflict Worksheet 3 117
    Day-to-Day Conflict Worksheet 4 124
    Day-to-Day Conflict Worksheet 5 131

Firefighting Situation Worksheet 2	138
Firefighting Situation Worksheet 3	149
Firefighting Situation Worksheet 4	160
Firefighting Situation Worksheet 5	171
Undesirable Effects Worksheet 2	182
Undesirable Effects Worksheet 3	189
Undesirable Effects Worksheet 4	196
Undesirable Effects Worksheet 5	203
Three-Cloud Approach Worksheet 2	210
Three-Cloud Approach Worksheet 3	233
Three-Cloud Approach Worksheet 4	256
Three-Cloud Approach Worksheet 5	279
Sources and Additional Reading	302

Introduction

Have you ever read The Goal by Elyahu Goaldratt? If the answer to that question is "No", stop reading this book immediately and go purchase and read that book. If the answer is yes, please proceed.

This is a workbook based on the work done on the Theory of Constraints by Elyahu Goldratt and others. It is the first iteration of a companion to the Theory of Constraints Handbook, as the handbook provides instructions but limited scaffolding for executing them. Given the complexity of the process and the self-referential nature of the processes, it's understandable that the team would net see it as essential to construct a workbook. However, I'm not a part of their team and my constraints don't dictate the same response.

You use this book by following the chapter instructions in the corresponding worksheet section. Each chapter is followed by a sample copy of the worksheet for that particular type of problem. The appendix of the book contains 4 additional copies of each worksheet. This makes this workbook a limited-use tool (unless you write in pencil and erase, which is advised).

But first, some necessary information!

This workbook has 5 basic applications, each associated with on of the major problem types. They are Inner Dilemmas, Day-to-Day Conflicts, Firefighting Situations, Undesirable effects, and the Three-Cloud Approach.

The Inner Dilemma process is for situations where we are conflicted between two choices. We can't do both, or think we can't, but there are good reasons for both.

The Day-To-Day Conflicts process exists to mediate the daily issues that happen between two people.

The Firefighting Situations process is for us in emergency scenarios where decisions have to be made to resolve the issue now and plans have to be made to prevent it from happening again in the future.

The Undesirable Effects process is for problem areas for which additional visibility or clarification is required to move toward resolution. This process is a generic version of all the others.

The Three-Cloud Approach process exists to tackle multiple, large scale Undesirable Effects at once. As problems in a single system, such as a business or government, often have common causes, they can also have common solutions.

Please keep in mind that these tools, when properly used, ARE silver bullets. No, that's not a typo. Yes, I meant to write "are". These are what you can consider to be "solve-all" methods. The drawback with them is that they are too long and laborious to go through for every single problem, though you can try if you want to. Going through these processes in earnest to attempt to solve problems is a cognitively challenging and time-consuming process and should be reserved from problems at a large scale and/or a high level of importance.

Lastly, you will see some jargon included in this book, such as 'cloud'. They originate with the Theory of Constraint methodology. If you want to know more about them, please review the additional resources section.

Good luck in solving your problems!

Silver Bullets

Section 1: Inner Dilemma

Inner Dilemma Solution Steps:

Step 1: Write the storyline.

Step 2: Write a list of considered actions, including that which you're under the most pressure to preform and what your preferred action would be.

Step 3: Build the Cloud.

What is the action that I feel under the most pressure to perform? Pick from the list of considered actions and write the answer in box D.

What is the action or decision that I prefer the most? Pick from the list of considered actions and write the answer in box E.

What do you need to perform D for? Write the answer in box B.

What need will not be met if E doesn't materialize? Write the answer in box C.

What won't happen without B and C? Write the answer in box A.

Step 4: Check and upgrade the Cloud.

Do you need to do D for B to happen? If yes, continue to the next question. If no, then think of something you need to do D for.

Is it impossible for C to happen without E? If yes, continue to the next question. If no, then think of some reason you need to do E.

Shane Ayers

Will doing D mean that you can't get C? If yes, continue to the next question. If no, then think of why you need C.

Will doing E mean that you have to give up on achieving B? If yes, continue to the next question. If no, then consider the need for B to occur.

In order to get to A, you need B and C? If yes, continue to the next step. If no, then think of some other central need that you must have both B and C to get.

Step 5: Surface assumptions.

Why can't A happen without B? Write the answer in box ABA.

Why can't A happen without C? Write the answer in box ACA.

Why can't B happen without D? Write the answer in box BDA.

Why can't C happen without E? Write the answer in box CEA.

Why can't B happen if E exists? Write the answer in box BEA.

Why can't C happen if D exists? Write the answer in box CDA.

Why can't you do D and E? Write the answer in box DEA.

Step 6: Construct the solution.

Can you change ABA in such a way that you can make A happen without B? If yes, write what you would change about ABA in box ABI. If no, move on to next question.

Can you change ACA in such a way that you can make A happen without C? If yes, write what you would change about ACA in box ACI. If no, move on to next question.

Silver Bullets

Can anything be done or changed about BDA so that you can achieve B without D? If yes, write what you would change about BDA in box BDI. If no, move on to next question.

Is there any way to change CEA so that you can get C without having to do E? If so, write what you would change about CEA in box CEI. If not, move on to next question.

How can you change DEA so that D and E can both be done? Write that in box DEI or move on.

That's it! You should now have at least one option for resolving your Internal Dilemma. Please revisit the checks in Steps 4 and 5 if you have reached the end of this exercise with no viable solutions.

Inner Dilemma Worksheet

Step 1.

Silver Bullets

Step 2.

I'm under pressure to
_____

I would much rather
_____

I feel under pressure because
_____

Considered Actions	Forced	Preferred

Shane Ayers

Step 3.

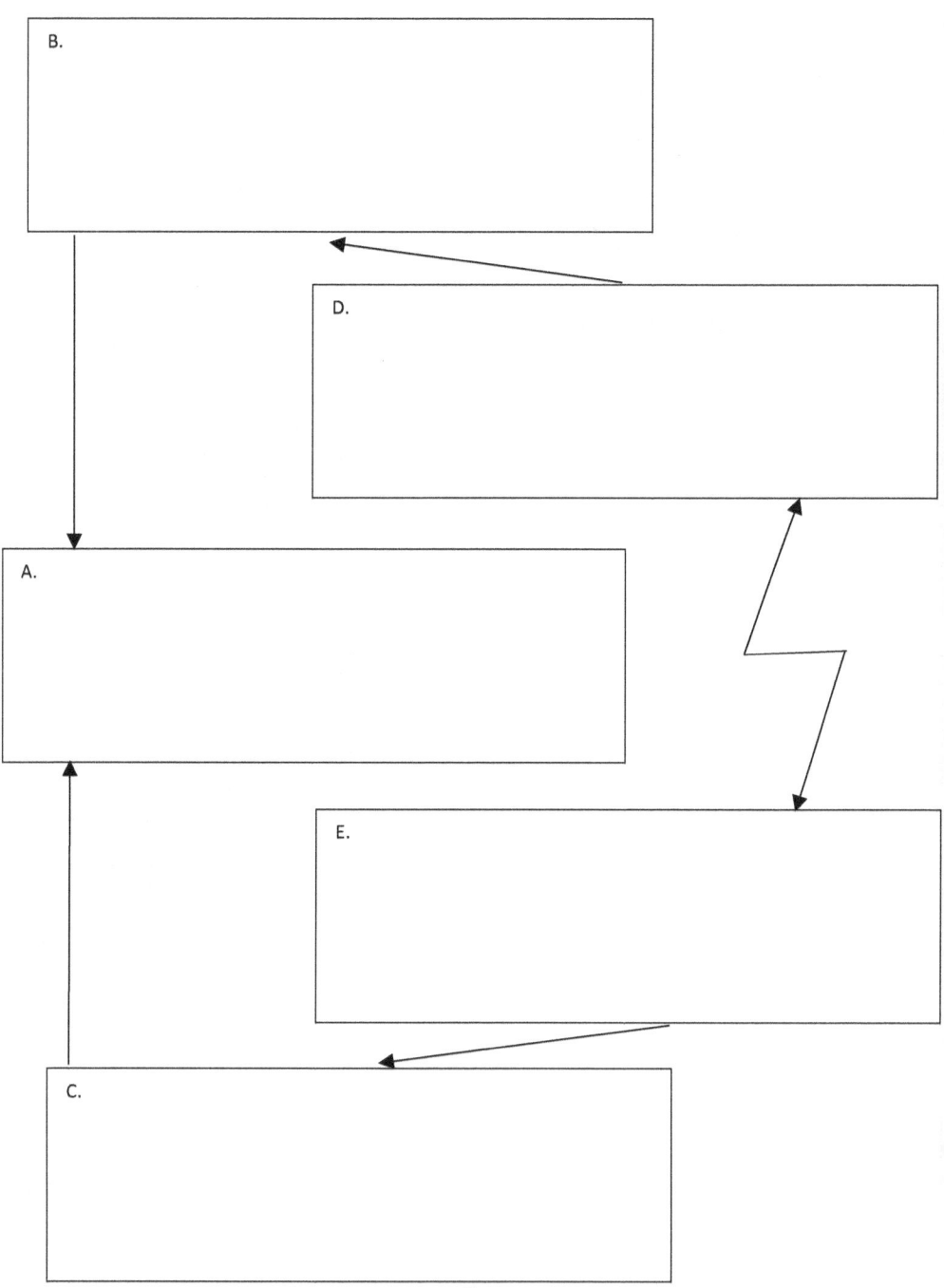

Silver Bullets

Step 5:

ABA

ACA

BDA

CEA

BEA

CDA

DEA

Silver Bullets

Step 6.

ABI

ACI

BDI

CEI

BEI

CDI

DEI

Section 2: Day-to-Day Conflicts
Day-to-Day Conflict Solution Steps

Step 1: Write the storyline.

Step 2: Build the Cloud.

What is the action or decision that the person you're in conflict with want to employ? Write that in box D.

What is the action or decision that you want to take? Write that in box E.

What is the need you're trying to satisfy by doing E? Write the need down in box C.

In your opinion, what need is the other person trying to satisfy by doing D? Write that down in box B.

What is the common objective that the other person and I collectively try to achieve by having B and C? Write that down in box A.

Step 3: Check and upgrade the Cloud.

Do you need to do D for B to happen? If yes, continue to the next question. If no, then think of something you need to do D for.

Is it impossible for C to happen without E? If yes, continue to the next question. If no, then think of some reason you need to do E.

Will doing D mean that you can't get C? If yes, continue to the next question. If no, then think of why you need C.

Will doing E mean that you have to give up on achieving B? If yes, continue to the next question. If no, then consider the need for B to occur.

In order to get to A, you need B and C? If yes, continue to the next step. If no, then think of some other central need that you must have both B and C to get.

Step 4: Surface assumptions.

Why can't A happen without B? Write the answer in box ABA.

Why can't A happen without C? Write the answer in box ACA.

Why can't B happen without D? Write the answer in box BDA.

Why can't C happen without E? Write the answer in box CEA.

Why can't B happen if E exists? Write the answer in box BEA.

Why can't C happen if D exists? Write the answer in box CDA.

Why can't you do D and E? Write the answer in box DEA.

Step 5: Construct the solution.

Can you change ABA in such a way that you can make A happen without B? If yes, write what you would change about ABA in box ABI. If no, move on to next question.

Can you change ACA in such a way that you can make A happen without C? If yes, write what you would change about ACA in box ACI. If no, move on to next question.

Silver Bullets

Can anything be done or changed about BDA so that you can achieve B without D? If yes, write what you would change about BDA in box BDI. If no, move on to next question.

Is there any way to change CEA so that you can get C without having to do E? If so, write what you would change about CEA in box CEI. If not, move on to next question.

How can you change DEA so that D and E can both be done? Write that in box DEI or move on to the next step.

Step 6: Communicate the solution.

Use the preferred solution box to write down the option from step 5 that you felt will best meet both your needs and resolve the conflict. Use the framework provided above that box to communicate on the subject.

Day-to-Day Conflict Worksheet

Step 1.

Silver Bullets

Step 2.

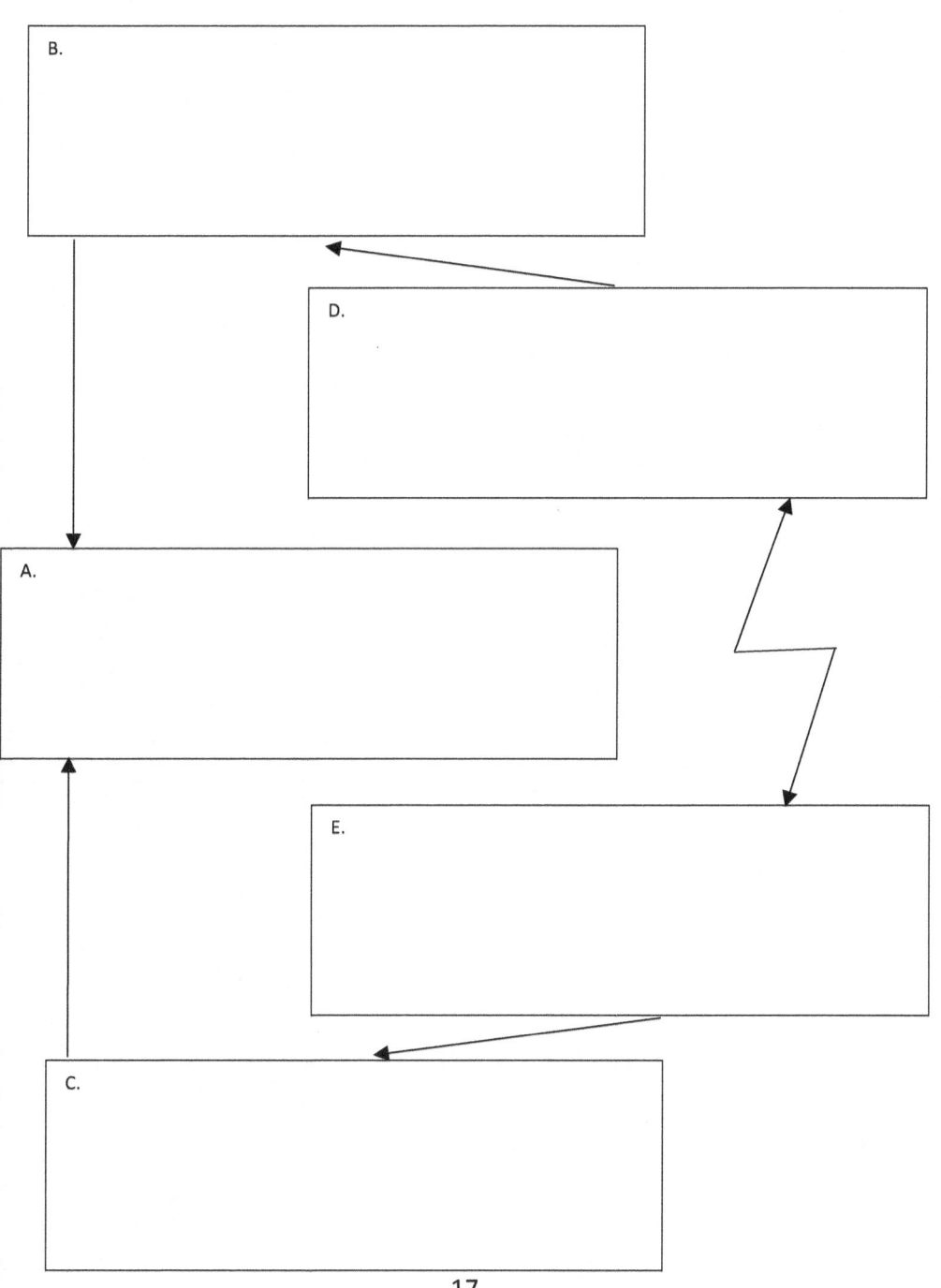

Step 4:

ABA

ACA

BDA

Silver Bullets

CEA

BEA

CDA

DEA

Step 5.

ABI

┌─────────────────────────────────────┐
│   │
│   │
│   │
│   │
└─────────────────────────────────────┘

ACI

┌─────────────────────────────────────┐
│   │
│   │
│   │
│   │
└─────────────────────────────────────┘

BDI

┌─────────────────────────────────────┐
│   │
│   │
│   │
│   │
└─────────────────────────────────────┘

Silver Bullets

CEI

BEI

CDI

DEI

Step 6.

Use the following script to present your solution to a Day-to-Day Conflict after selecting which of the entries for Step 6 you would prefer to use.

Preferred solution for a day-to-day conflict:

```
[                                                    ]
```

Script: We have a difference of opinions on the issue of . . . I have been thinking about it and I would like to work with you on finding a workable solution. You want D and I want D'. These two are not compatible. I suggest we go with your D but we need to ensure that my C is taken care of as well. Do you have any suggestion how we can take care of it?

Section 3: Firefighting Situations
Firefighting Situation Solution Steps

Step 1: Write the storyline.

Step 2: Build the Cloud.

What important need of the system does this emergency put in danger? Write that in box B.

What action can be taken to meet the need in B? Write that in box D.

What action or procedure is in place that prevents taking the action in box D? Write the need down in box E.

What other important need of the system demands the procedure that is stated in E? Write that down in box C.

What is the common objective achieved by having B and C? Write that down in box A.

Step 3: Check and upgrade the Cloud.

Do you need to do D for B to happen? If yes, continue to the next question. If no, then think of something you need to do D for.

Is it impossible for C to happen without E? If yes, continue to the next question. If no, then think of some reason you need to do E.

Will doing D mean that you can't get C? If yes, continue to the next question. If no, then think of why you need C.

Will doing E mean that you have to give up on achieving B? If yes, continue to the next question. If no, then consider the need for B to occur.

In order to get to A, you need B and C? If yes, continue to the next step. If no, then think of some other central need that you must have both B and C to get.

Step 4: Surface assumptions.

Why can't A happen without B? Write the answer in box ABA.

Why can't A happen without C? Write the answer in box ACA.

Why can't B happen without D? Write the answer in box BDA.

Why can't C happen without E? Write the answer in box CEA.

Why can't B happen if E exists? Write the answer in box BEA.

Why can't C happen if D exists? Write the answer in box CDA.

Why can't you do D and E? Write the answer in box DEA.

Step 5: Construct the solution.

Can anything be done or changed about BDA so that you can achieve B without D? If yes, write what you would change about BDA in box BDI. If no, move on to next question.

Is there any way to change CEA so that you can get C without having to do E? If so, write what you would change about CEA in box CEI. If not, move on to next question.

How can you change DEA so that D and E can both be done? Write that in box DEI or move on to the next question.

Silver Bullets

Is there a way for you to take any of the entries in BDI, CEI or DEI and use it to fix the entire situation? Can you satisfy B and C both that way? Write that in the combined solution for a firefighting conflict box. That's your solution.

Step 6: Communicate the solution.

Copy boxes A-E from Step 2 to the communication sheet..

Present the entities of the cloud to the person who raised the problem in the following order: A,B,D and then A,C,E. Get agreement and take any notes.

Present the entities of the cloud to the key person the procedure is associated with in the following order: A,C,E and then A,B,D. Get agreement and take any notes.

Modify your original solution as needed or replace with superior solution suggested by parties that satisfies the system needs (A, B and C).

Shane Ayers

Firefighting Situation Worksheet

Step 1.

Silver Bullets

Step 3.

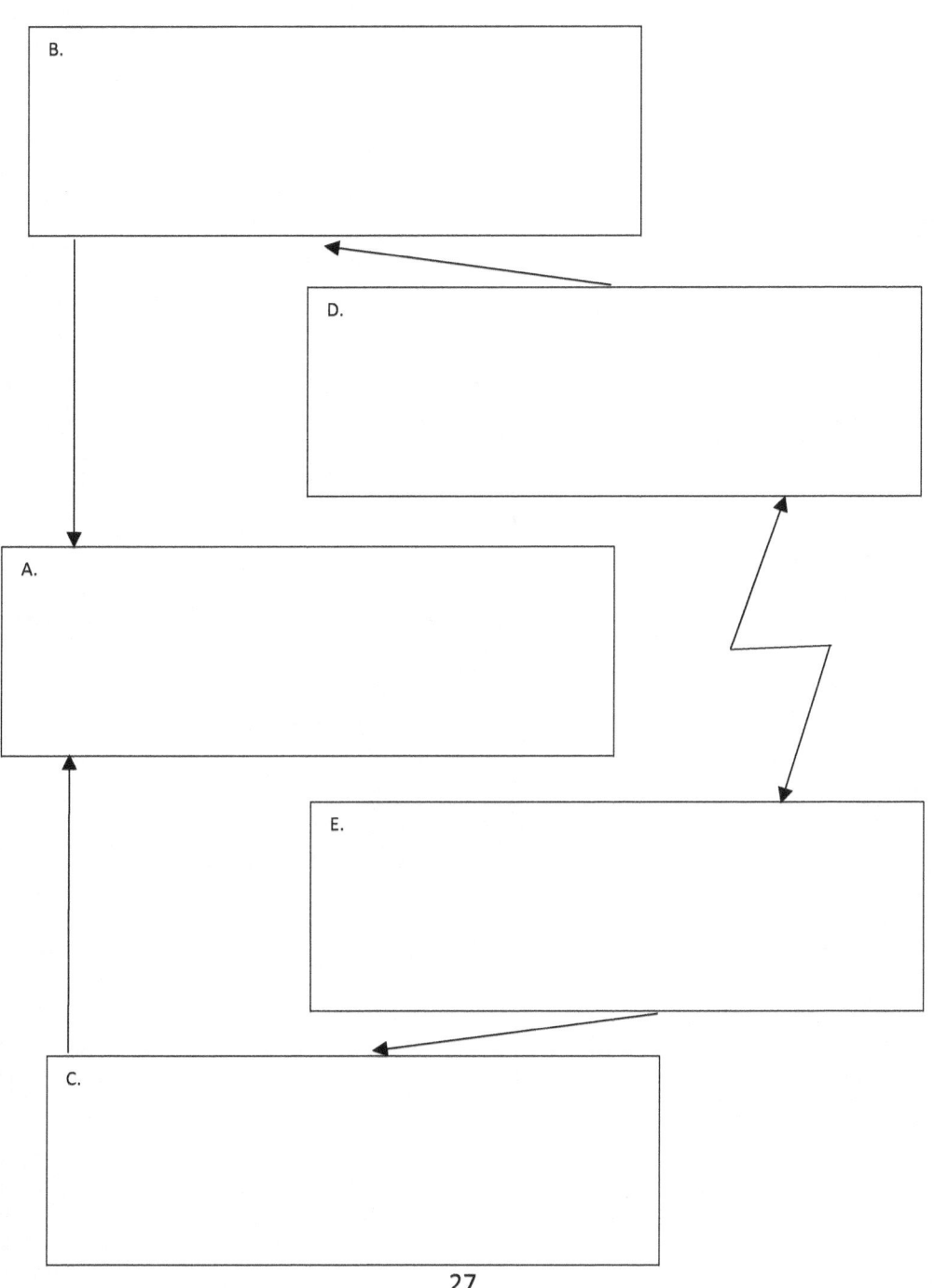

Step 5:

ABA

ACA

BDA

Silver Bullets

CEA

BEA

CDA

DEA

Step 6.

ABI

ACI

BDI

Silver Bullets

CEI

BEI

CDI

DEI

Shane Ayers

Combined solution for a firefighting conflict:

A

B

C

D

E

Silver Bullets

Notes from person who raised the problem:

Alternate solution from person who raised the problem:

Silver Bullets

Notes from the key person associated with the procedure:

Alternate solution from the key person associated with the procedure:

Section 4: Undesirable Effects
Undesirable Effects Solution Steps

Step 1: Identify UDE

Must have the following qualities:

- It has negative implications on the performance of the system.
- It has been in existence for a length of time (at least several months).
- There have been attempts to sort it out with little or no success.

Step 2: Eliminate or rewrite if it has any of the following qualities:

- It is a complaint about an ongoing problem that exists in your reality and because of this problem, you cannot perform better. It should be written in present tense.
- It is a description of the state, not an action.
- It is within your area of responsibility.
- Something can be done about it.
- It must not blame someone.
- It must not be a speculated cause.
- It must not be a hidden solution to the problem (wishful thinking of solving the problem).
- It should contain one entity.
- It should not include its cause in its verbalization.
- It should be factual and not subjective.
- It should be a complete sentence.

Step 3: Write the storyline

Step 4: Build the UDE Cloud.

Why is this UDE undesirable? What important need of the system does it jeopardize or endanger? Write in box B.

What action should be taken to meet the jeopardized need in B? Write in box D.

What other important need prevents you from always taking the action D? Write in box C.

What action do you take to meet the need in C? Write in box E.

What is the common objective achieved with both B and C? Write in box A.

Step 5: Check and upgrade the Cloud.

Do you need to do D for B to happen? If yes, continue to the next question. If no, then think of something you need to do D for.

Is it impossible for C to happen without E? If yes, continue to the next question. If no, then think of some reason you need to do E.

Will doing D mean that you can't get C? If yes, continue to the next question. If no, then think of why you need C.

Will doing E mean that you have to give up on achieving B? If yes, continue to the next question. If no, then consider the need for B to occur.

In order to get to A, you need B and C? If yes, continue to the next step. If no, then think of some other central need that you must have both B and C to get.

Silver Bullets

Step 6: Surface assumptions.

Why can't A happen without B? Write the answer in box ABA.

Why can't A happen without C? Write the answer in box ACA.

Why can't B happen without D? Write the answer in box BDA.

Why can't C happen without E? Write the answer in box CEA.

Why can't B happen if E exists? Write the answer in box BEA.

Why can't C happen if D exists? Write the answer in box CDA.

Why can't you do D and E? Write the answer in box DEA.

Step 7: Construct the solution.

Can you change ABA in such a way that you can make A happen without B? If yes, write what you would change about ABA in box ABI. If no, move on to next question.

Can you change ACA in such a way that you can make A happen without C? If yes, write what you would change about ACA in box ACI. If no, move on to next question.

Can anything be done or changed about BDA so that you can achieve B without D? If yes, write what you would change about BDA in box BDI. If no, move on to next question.

Is there any way to change CEA so that you can get C without having to do E? If so, write what you would change about CEA in box CEI. If not, move on to next question.

How can you change DEA so that D and E can both be done? Write that in box DEI or move on to the next question.

Step 8: Communicate the solution.

Present the entities of the cloud and get agreement on all of them and their connections. Revise as necessary. Get commitment to finding a win-win solution. Then present your best change from step 7, explaining how it resolves the UDE.

Silver Bullets

Undesirable Effects Worksheet

Step 1.

Step 3.

Step 4.

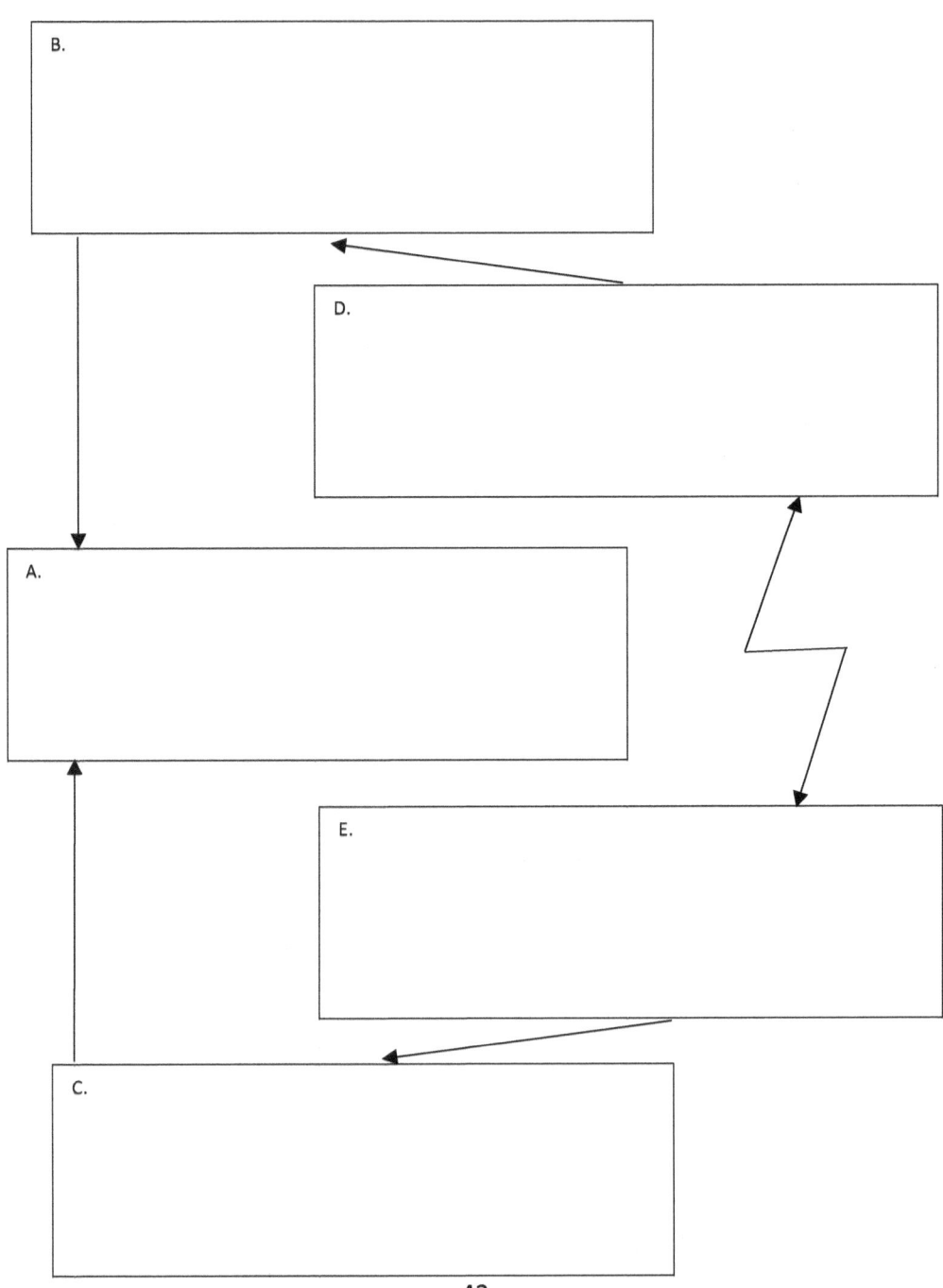

Silver Bullets

Step 6:

ABA

ACA

BDA

CEA

BEA

CDA

DEA

Silver Bullets

Step 7.

ABI

ACI

BDI

CEI

BEI

CDI

DEI

Silver Bullets

Step 8

A

B

C

D

E

Section 5: Three-Cloud Approach
Three-Cloud Approach Solution Steps

Step 1: Identify 3 UDEs

Each must have the following qualities:

- It has negative implications on the performance of the system.
- It has been in existence for a length of time (at least several months).
- There have been attempts to sort it out with little or no success.
- Must be a complete sentence

Step 2: Eliminate or rewrite if any have any of the following qualities:

- It is a complaint about an ongoing problem that exists in your reality and because of this problem, you cannot perform better. It should be written in present tense.
- It is a description of the state, not an action.
- It is within your area of responsibility.
- Something can be done about it.
- It must not blame someone.
- It must not be a speculated cause.
- It must not be a hidden solution to the problem (wishful thinking of solving the problem).
- It should contain one entity.
- It should not include its cause in its verbalization.
- It should be factual and not subjective.
- It should be a complete sentence.

Each should be a complete sentence.

Step 3a: Write the storyline for UDE 1

Silver Bullets

Step 4a: Build the UDE Cloud for UDE 1

Why is this UDE undesirable? What important need of the system does it jeopardize or endanger? Write in box B1.

What action should be taken to meet the jeopardized need in B? Write in box D1.

What other important need prevents you from always taking the action D1? Write in box C1.

What action do you take to meet the need in C1? Write in box E1.

What is the common objective achieved with both B1 and C1? Write in box A1.

Step 5a: Check and upgrade the Cloud for UDE 1

Do you need to do D1 for B1 to happen? If yes, continue to the next question. If no, then think of something you need to do D1 for.

Is it impossible for C1 to happen without E1? If yes, continue to the next question. If no, then think of some reason you need to do E1.

Will doing D1 mean that you can't get C1? If yes, continue to the next question. If no, then think of why you need C1.

Will doing E1 mean that you have to give up on achieving B1? If yes, continue to the next question. If no, then consider the need for B1 to occur.

In order to get to A1, you need B1 and C1? If yes, continue to the next step. If no, then think of some other central need that you must have both B1 and C1 to get.

Step 6a: Surface assumptions.

Why can't A1 happen without B1? Write the answer in box ABA1.

Why can't A1 happen without C1? Write the answer in box ACA1.

Why can't B1 happen without D1? Write the answer in box BDA1.

Why can't C1 happen without E1? Write the answer in box CEA1.

Why can't B1 happen if E1 exists? Write the answer in box BEA1.

Why can't C1 happen if D1 exists? Write the answer in box CDA1.

Why can't you do D1 and E1? Write the answer in box DEA1.

Step 3b: Write the storyline for UDE 2

Step 4b: Build the UDE Cloud for UDE 2

Why is this UDE undesirable? What important need of the system does it jeopardize or endanger? Write in box B2.

What action should be taken to meet the jeopardized need in B2? Write in box D2.

What other important need prevents you from always taking the action D2? Write in box C2.

What action do you take to meet the need in C2? Write in box E2.

What is the common objective achieved with both B2 and C2? Write in box A2.

Step 5b: Check and upgrade the Cloud for UDE 2

Silver Bullets

Do you need to do D2 for B2 to happen? If yes, continue to the next question. If no, then think of something you need to do D2 for.

Is it impossible for C2 to happen without E2? If yes, continue to the next question. If no, then think of some reason you need to do E2.

Will doing D2 mean that you can't get C2? If yes, continue to the next question. If no, then think of why you need C2.

Will doing E2 mean that you have to give up on achieving B2? If yes, continue to the next question. If no, then consider the need for B2 to occur.

In order to get to A2, you need B2 and C2? If yes, continue to the next step. If no, then think of some other central need that you must have both B2 and C2 to get.

Step 6b: Surface assumptions.

Why can't A2 happen without B2? Write the answer in box ABA2.

Why can't A2 happen without C2? Write the answer in box ACA2.

Why can't B2 happen without D2? Write the answer in box BDA2.

Why can't C2 happen without E2? Write the answer in box CEA2.

Why can't B2 happen if E2 exists? Write the answer in box BEA2.

Why can't C2 happen if D2 exists? Write the answer in box CDA2.

Why can't you do D2 and E2? Write the answer in box DEA2.

Step 3c: Write the storyline for UDE 3

Step 4c: Build the UDE Cloud for UDE 3

Why is this UDE undesirable? What important need of the system does it jeopardize or endanger? Write in box B3.

What action should be taken to meet the jeopardized need in B3? Write in box D3.

What other important need prevents you from always taking the action D3? Write in box C3.

What action do you take to meet the need in C3? Write in box E3.

What is the common objective achieved with both B3 and C3? Write in box A3.

Step 5c: Check and upgrade the Cloud for UDE 3

Do you need to do D3 for B3 to happen? If yes, continue to the next question. If no, then think of something you need to do D3 for.

Is it impossible for C3 to happen without E3? If yes, continue to the next question. If no, then think of some reason you need to do E3.

Will doing D3 mean that you can't get C3? If yes, continue to the next question. If no, then think of why you need C3.

Will doing E3 mean that you have to give up on achieving B3? If yes, continue to the next question. If no, then consider the need for B3 to occur.

In order to get to A3, you need B3 and C3? If yes, continue to the next step. If no, then think of some other central need that you must have both B3 and C3 to get.

Step 6c: Surface assumptions.

Why can't A3 happen without B3? Write the answer in box ABA3.

Silver Bullets

Why can't A3 happen without C3? Write the answer in box ACA3.

Why can't B3 happen without D3? Write the answer in box BDA3.

Why can't C3 happen without E3? Write the answer in box CEA3.

Why can't B3 happen if E3 exists? Write the answer in box BEA3.

Why can't C3 happen if D3 exists? Write the answer in box CDA3.

Why can't you do D3 and E3? Write the answer in box DEA3.

Step 7: Consolidate the cloud.

Combine A1, A2, and A3 into a single sentence that covers all 3 in a generic manner. Write in box Generic A.

Combine B1, B2, and B3 into a single sentence that covers all 3 in a generic manner. Write in box Generic B.

Combine C1, C2, and C3 into a single sentence that covers all 3 in a generic manner. Write in box Generic C.

Combine D1, D2, and D3 into a single sentence that covers all 3 in a generic manner. Write in box Generic D.

Combine E1, E2, and E3 into a single sentence that covers all 3 in a generic manner. Write in box Generic E.

You may need to 'flip' one or more of the clouds, turning B and D into C and E and vice versa, depending on what perspective each cloud was written from.

Take another UDE, develop the UDE Cloud for it, and check if the Cloud fits the pattern of the Consolidated Cloud. A fit means that A, B, and C are about the same verbalization and D and D' are of the same nature of the D and D' of Consolidated Cloud.

Step 8. Surface assumptions of the consolidated cloud.

Why can't Generic A happen without Generic B? Write the answer in box Generic ABA.

Why can't Generic A happen without Generic C? Write the answer in box Generic ACA.

Why can't Generic B happen without Generic D? Write the answer in box Generic BDA.

Why can't Generic C happen without Generic E? Write the answer in box Generic CEA.

Why can't Generic B happen if Generic E exists? Write the answer in box Generic BEA.

Why can't Generic C happen if Generic D exists? Write the answer in box Generic CDA.

Why can't you do Generic D and Generic E? Write the answer in box Generic DEA.

Step 9. Construct the generic solution.

Can you change Generic ABA in such a way that you can make Generic A happen without Generic B? If yes, write what you would change about Generic ABA in box Generic ABI. If no, move on to next question.

Can you change Generic ACA in such a way that you can make Generic A happen without Generic C? If yes, write what you would

Silver Bullets

change about Generic ACA in box Generic ACI. If no, move on to next question.

Can anything be done or changed about Generic BDA so that you can achieve Generic B without Generic D? If yes, write what you would change about Generic BDA in box Generic BDI. If no, move on to next question.

Is there any way to change Generic CEA so that you can get Generic C without having to do Generic E? If so, write what you would change about Generic CEA in box Generic CEI. If not, move on to next question.

How can you change Generic DEA so that Generic D and Generic E can both be done? Write that in box Generic DEI or move on to the next step.

Step 10: Construct individual solutions to pair with the generic solutions for the individual UDE clouds, based on the generic solutions:

Compare Generic ABI, Generic ACI, Generic BDI, Generic CEI and Generic DEI to the ABA, ACA, BDA, CEA, BEA, and DEA of the individual UDE you're trying to solve. See if any of those generic solutions can be easily adapted to resolve those entries. Enter the adapted solution in the appropriate Adapted solution box.

Step 11: Communicate the solution.

Present the entities of the generic cloud and get agreement on all of them and their connections. Revise as necessary. Get commitment to finding a win-win solution. Then present your best change from step 10, explaining how it resolves the problem.

Three-Cloud Approach Worksheet
Step 1.

Silver Bullets

Step 3a.

Step 4a.

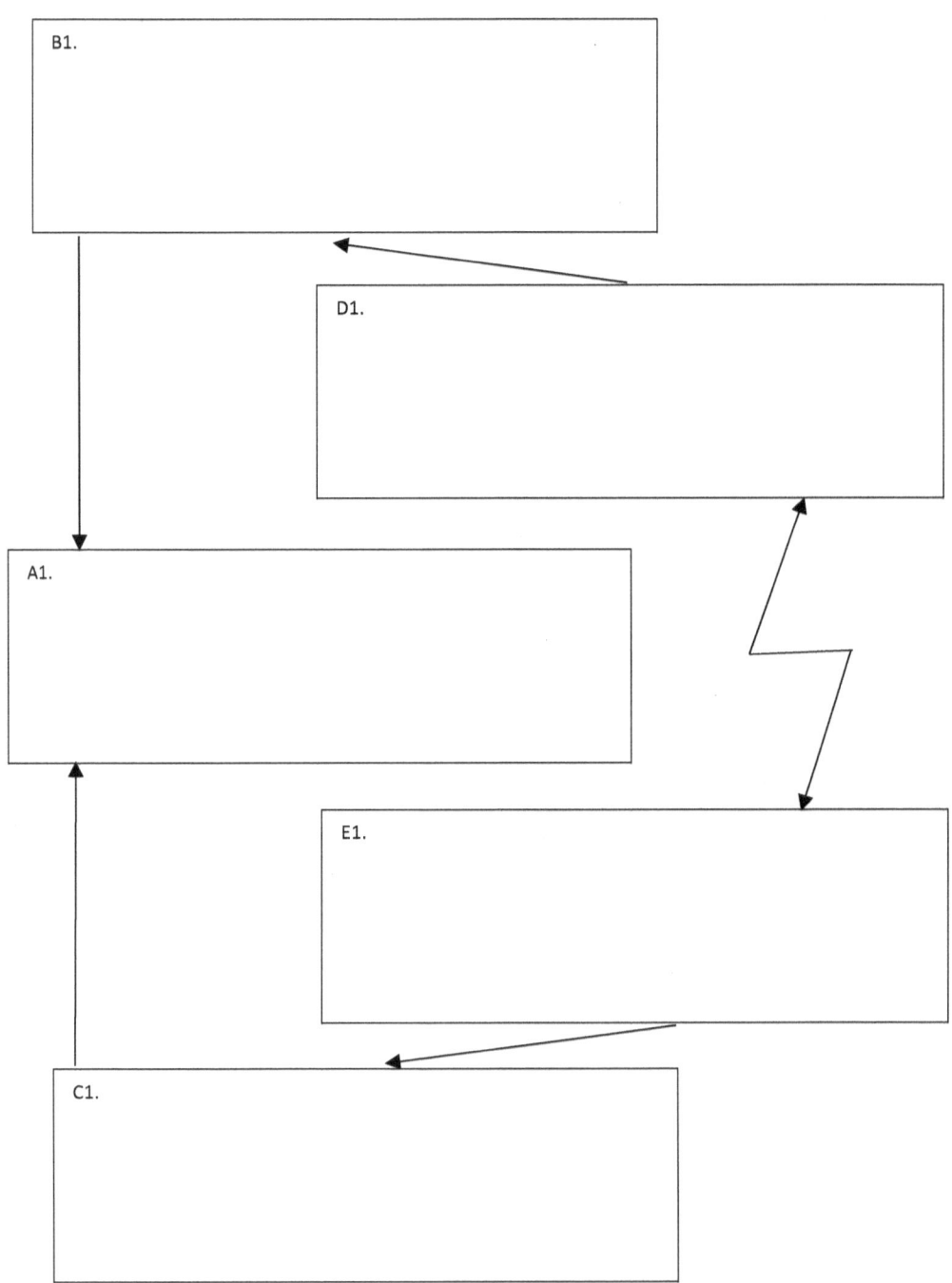

Silver Bullets

Step 6a:

ABA1

ACA1

BDA1

CEA1

```
┌─────────────────────────────────────────────────┐
│                                                 │
│                                                 │
│                                                 │
│                                                 │
└─────────────────────────────────────────────────┘
```

BEA1

```
┌─────────────────────────────────────────────────┐
│                                                 │
│                                                 │
│                                                 │
│                                                 │
└─────────────────────────────────────────────────┘
```

CDA1

```
┌─────────────────────────────────────────────────┐
│                                                 │
│                                                 │
│                                                 │
│                                                 │
└─────────────────────────────────────────────────┘
```

DEA1

```
┌─────────────────────────────────────────────────┐
│                                                 │
│                                                 │
│                                                 │
│                                                 │
└─────────────────────────────────────────────────┘
```

Silver Bullets

Step 3b.

Step 4b.

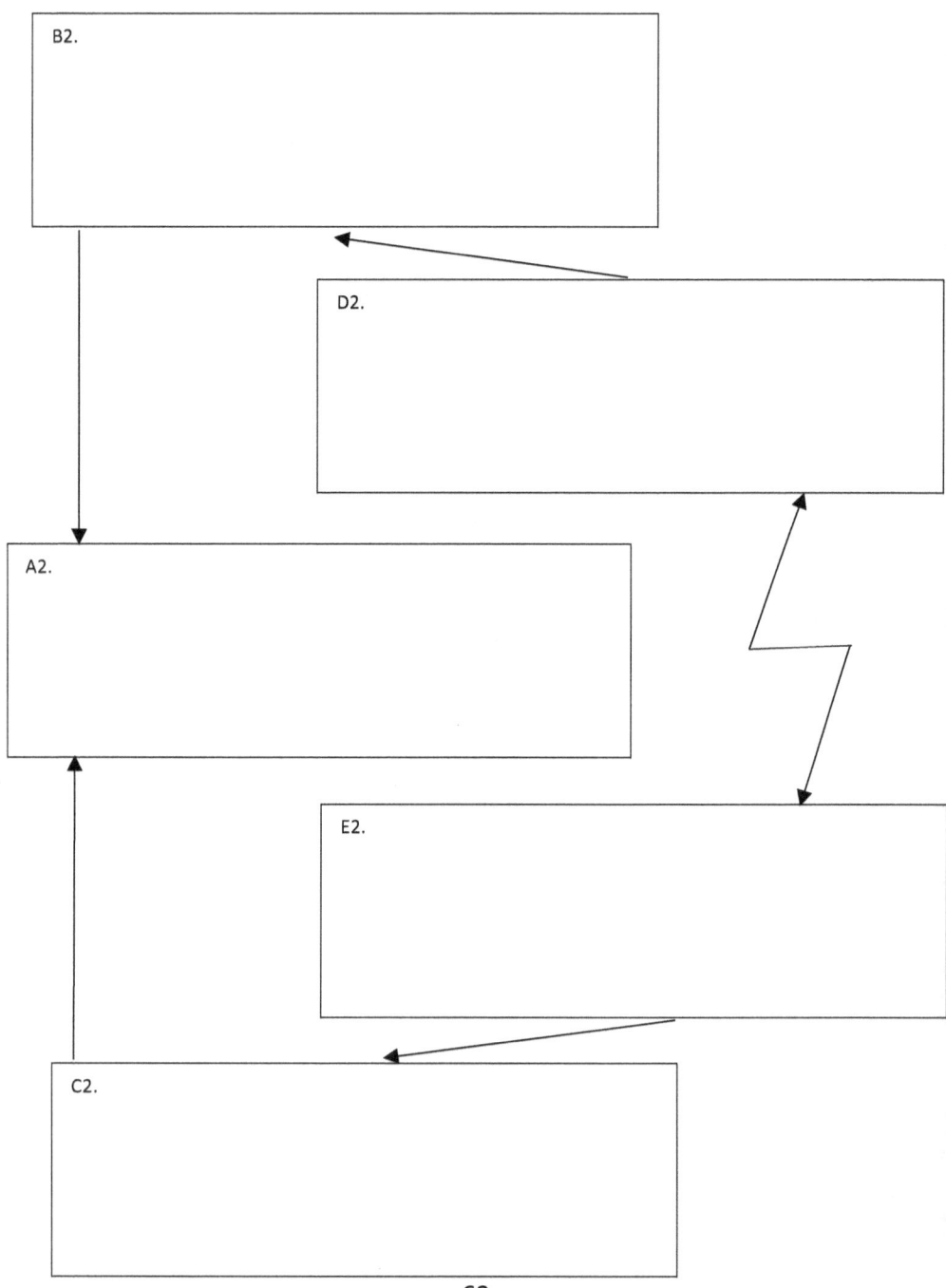

Silver Bullets

Step 6b:

ABA2

ACA2

BDA2

CEA2

BEA2

CDA2

DEA2

Silver Bullets

Step 3c.

Step 4c.

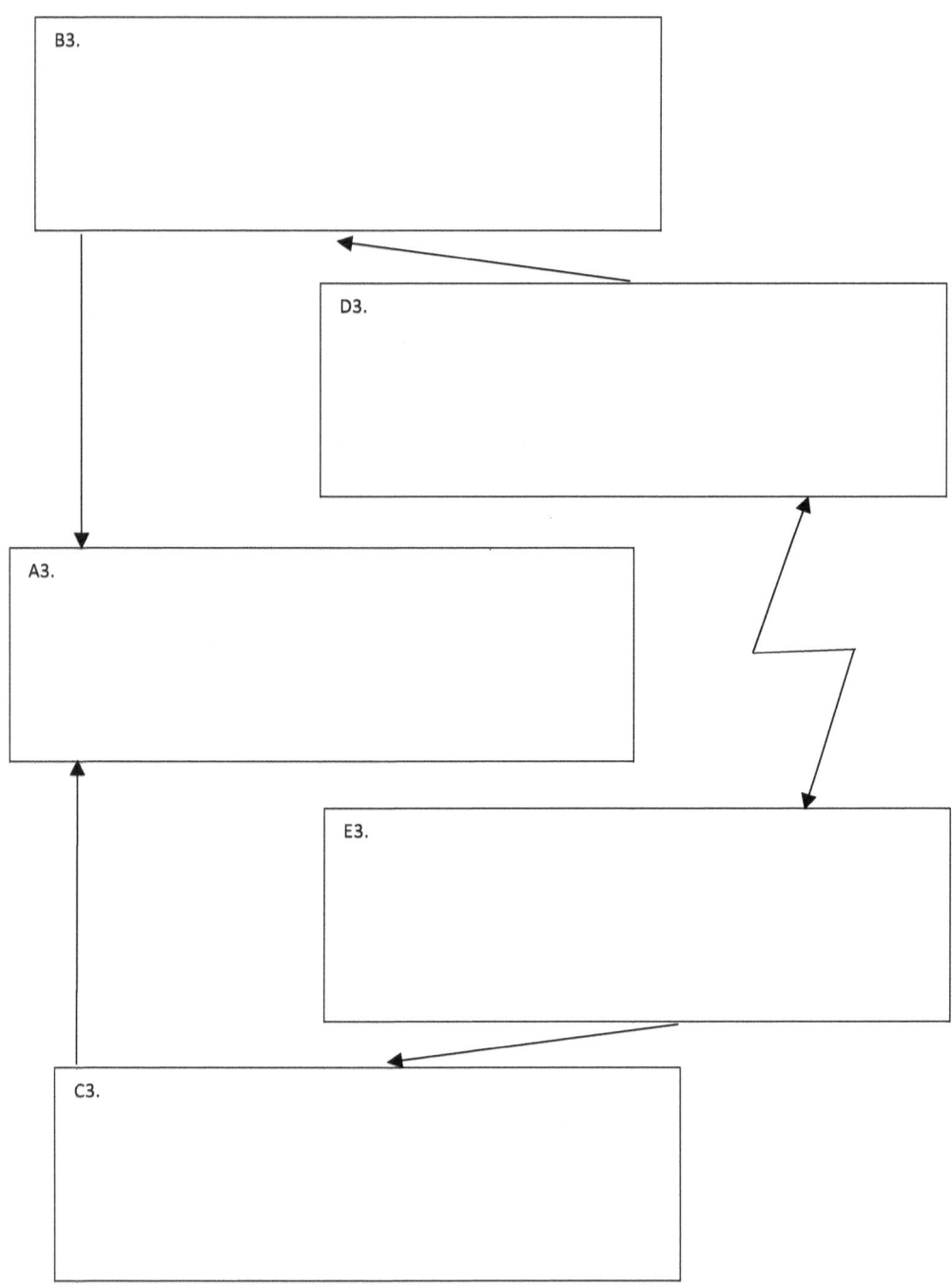

Silver Bullets

Step 6a:

ABA3

ACA3

BDA3

CEA3

BEA3

CDA3

DEA3

Silver Bullets

Step 7.

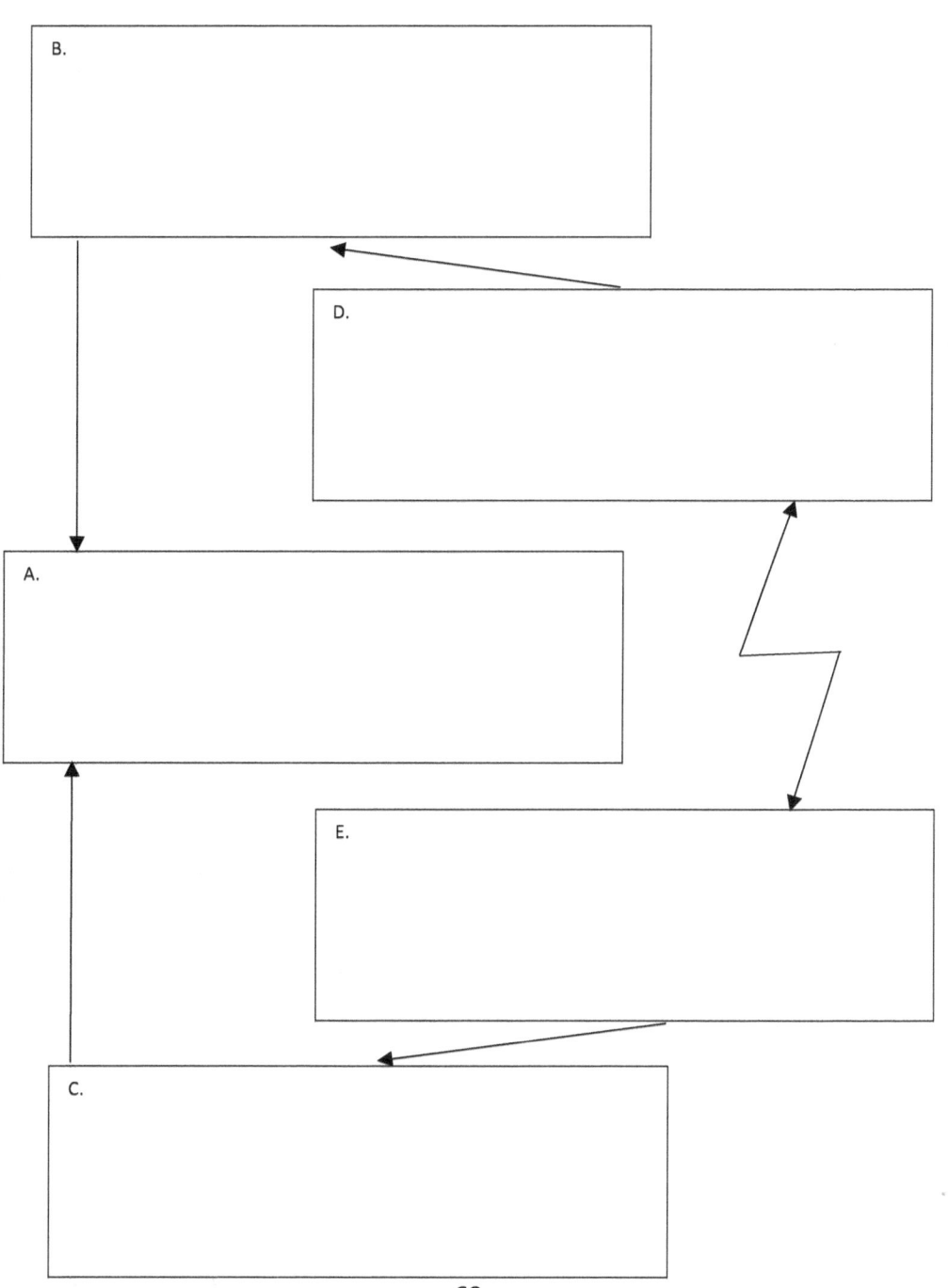

Step 8:

Generic ABA

Generic ACA

Generic BDA

Silver Bullets

Generic CEA

Generic BEA

Generic CDA

Generic DEA

Step 9.

Generic ABI

Generic ACI

Generic BDI

Silver Bullets

Generic CEI

Generic BEI

Generic CDI

Generic DEI

Step 10a.

Adapted ABI for UDE 1

Adapted ACI for UDE 1

Adapted BDI for UDE 1

Adapted CEI for UDE 1

Silver Bullets

Adapted BEI for UDE 1

Adapted CDI for UDE 1

Adapted DEI for UDE 1

Step 10a.

Adapted ABI for UDE 2

Adapted ACI for UDE 2

Adapted BDI for UDE 2

Adapted CEI for UDE 2

Silver Bullets

Adapted BEI for UDE 2

Adapted CDI for UDE 2

Adapted DEI for UDE 2

Step 10a.

Adapted ABI for UDE 3

Adapted ACI for UDE 3

Adapted BDI for UDE 3

Adapted CEI for UDE 3

Silver Bullets

Adapted BEI for UDE 3

Adapted CDI for UDE 3

Adapted DEI for UDE 3

Shane Ayers

Communication Sheet

Adapted Three-Cloud Approach Solution:

Generic A

Generic B

Generic C

Generic D

Generic E

Appendix: Worksheets

Inner Dilemma Worksheet 2

Step 1.

Silver Bullets

Step 2.

I'm under pressure to
_____

I would much rather
_____

I feel under pressure because
_____

Considered Actions	Forced	Preferred

Step 3.

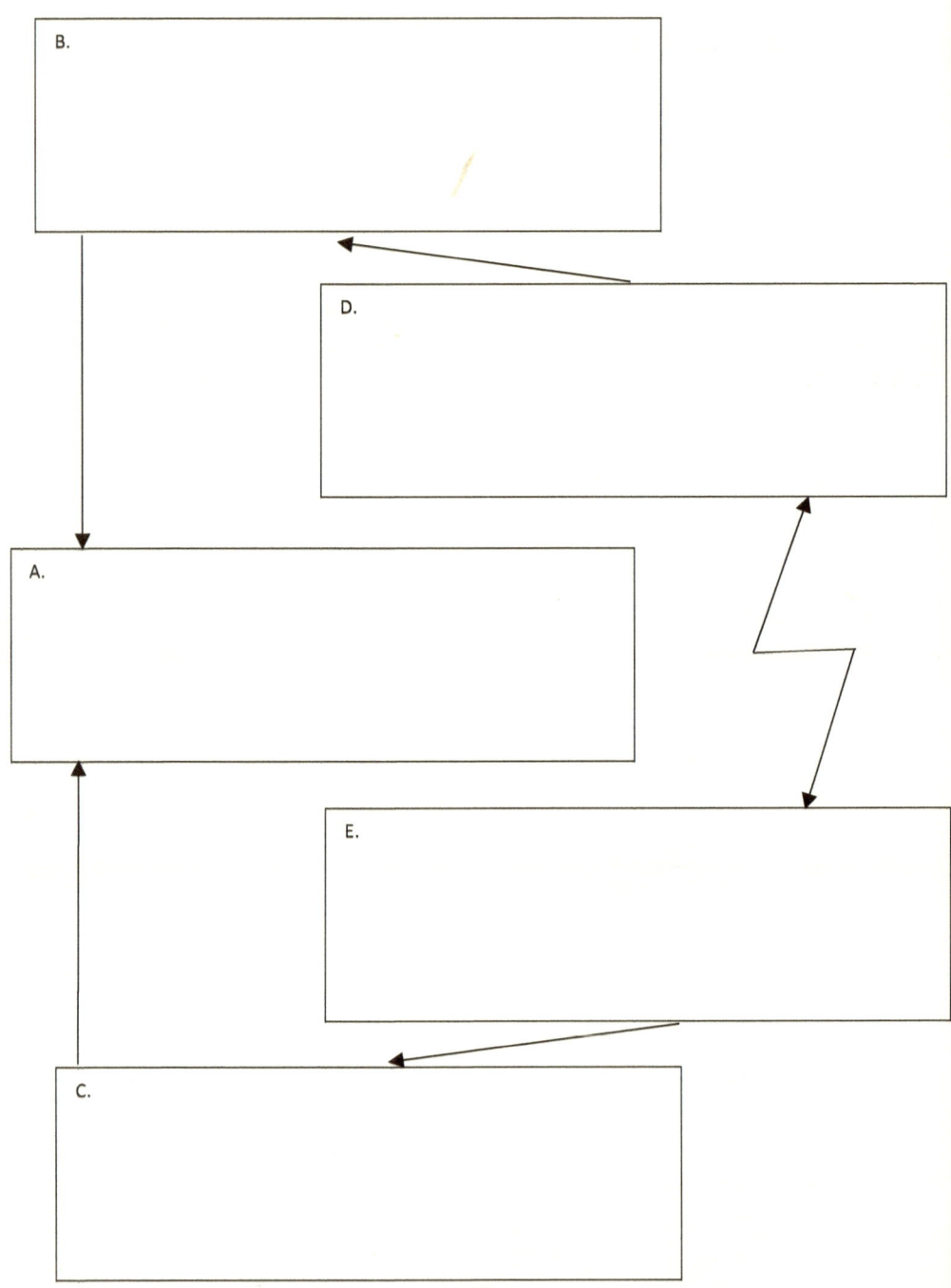

Silver Bullets

Step 5:

ABA

ACA

BDA

Shane Ayers

CEA

BEA

CDA

DEA

Silver Bullets

Step 6.

ABI

ACI

BDI

CEI

BEI

CDI

DEI

Silver Bullets

Inner Dilemma Worksheet 3

Step 1.

Step 2.

I'm under pressure to
_____

I would much rather
_____

I feel under pressure because
_____

Considered Actions	Forced	Preferred

Silver Bullets

Step 3.

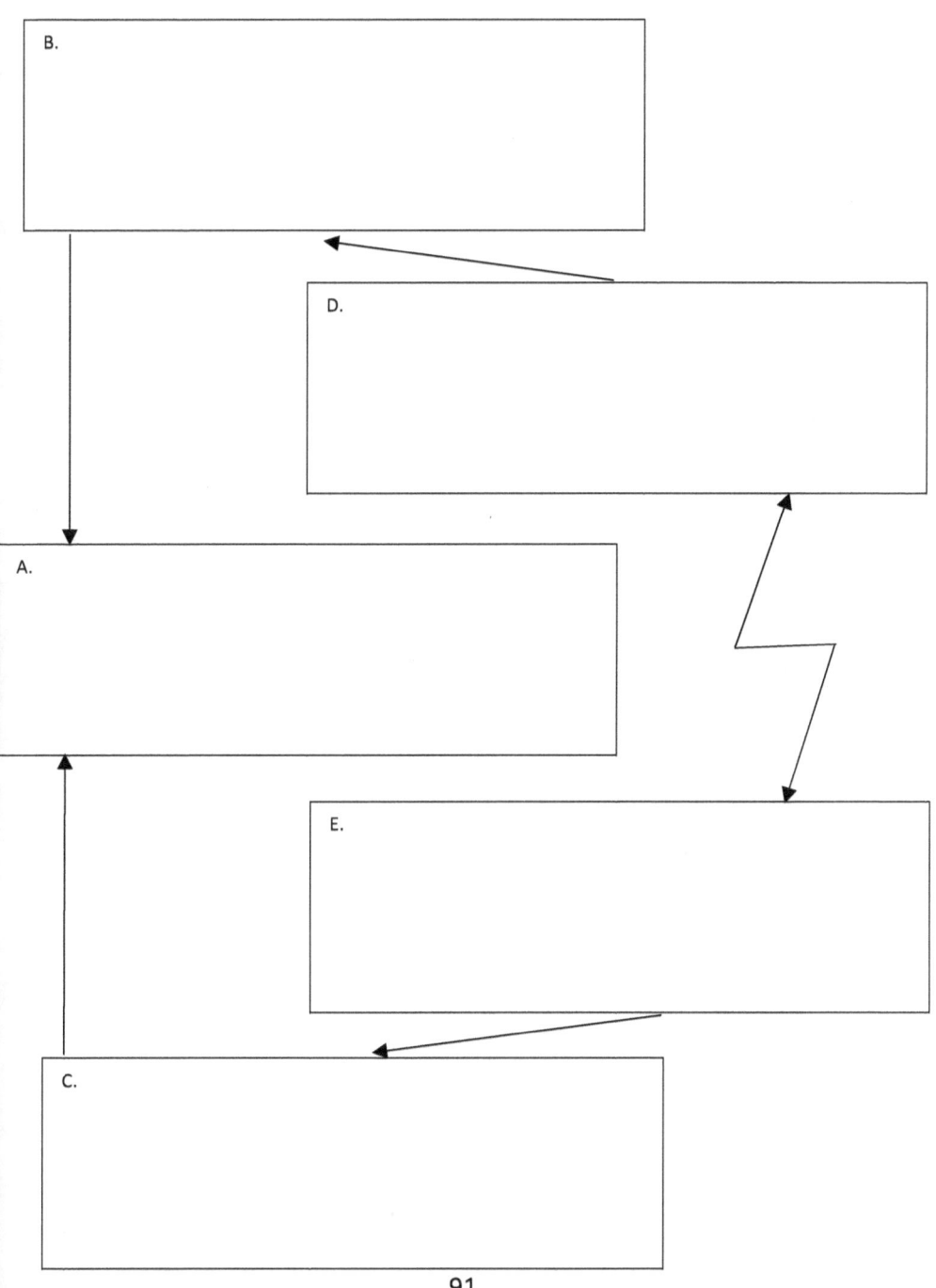

Step 5:

ABA

ACA

BDA

Silver Bullets

CEA

BEA

CDA

DEA

Step 6.

ABI

ACI

BDI

Silver Bullets

CEI

BEI

CDI

DEI

Shane Ayers

Inner Dilemma Worksheet 4

Step 1.

Silver Bullets

Step 2.

I'm under pressure to
_____

I would much rather

_____

I feel under pressure because

_____

Considered Actions	Forced	Preferred

Step 3.

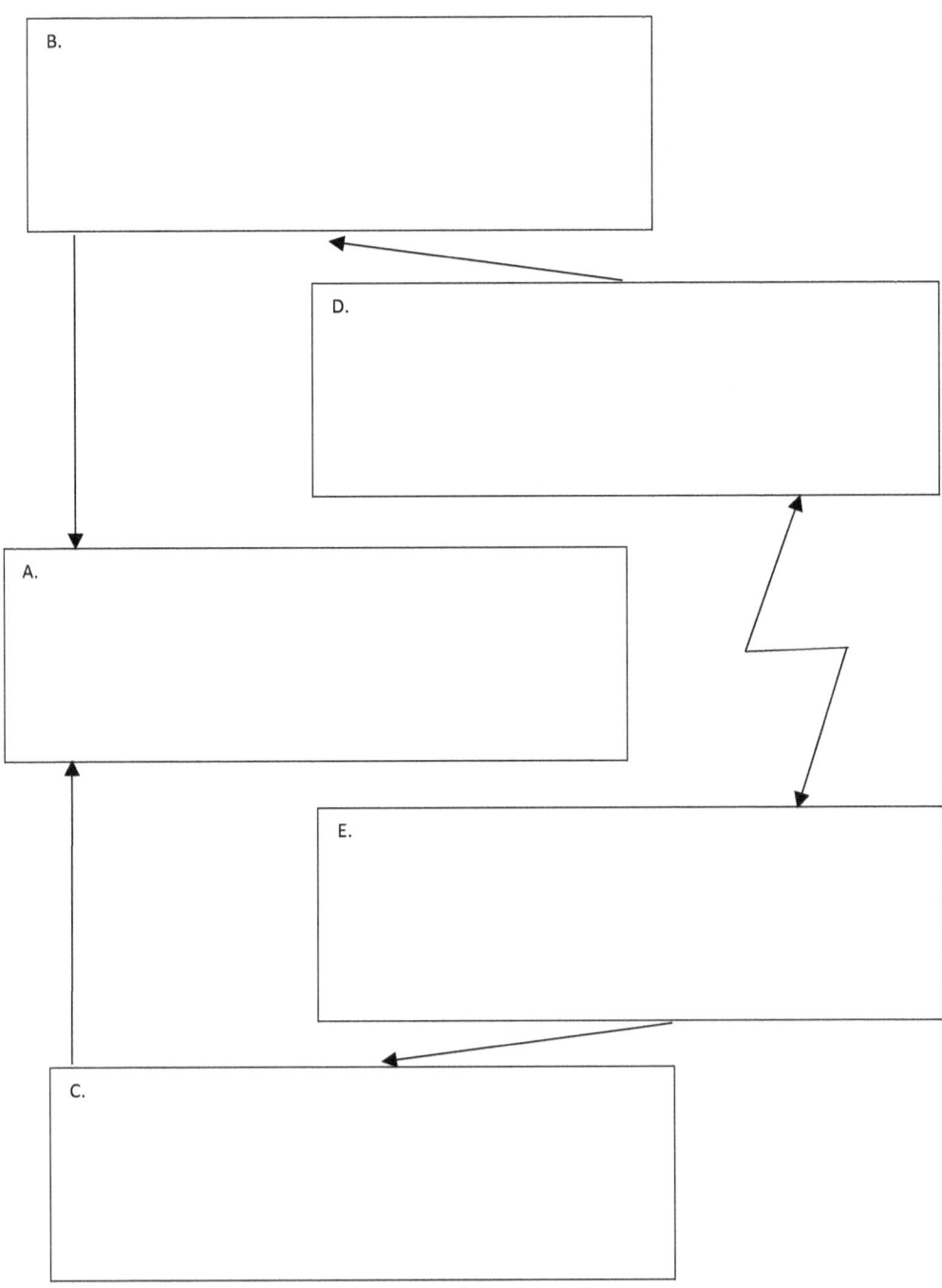

Silver Bullets

Step 5:

ABA

ACA

BDA

CEA

BEA

CDA

DEA

Silver Bullets

Step 6.

ABI

ACI

BDI

CEI

BEI

CDI

DEI

Silver Bullets

Inner Dilemma Worksheet 5

Step 1.

Step 2.

I'm under pressure to
_____

I would much rather
_____

I feel under pressure because
_____

Considered Actions	Forced	Preferred

Silver Bullets

Step 3.

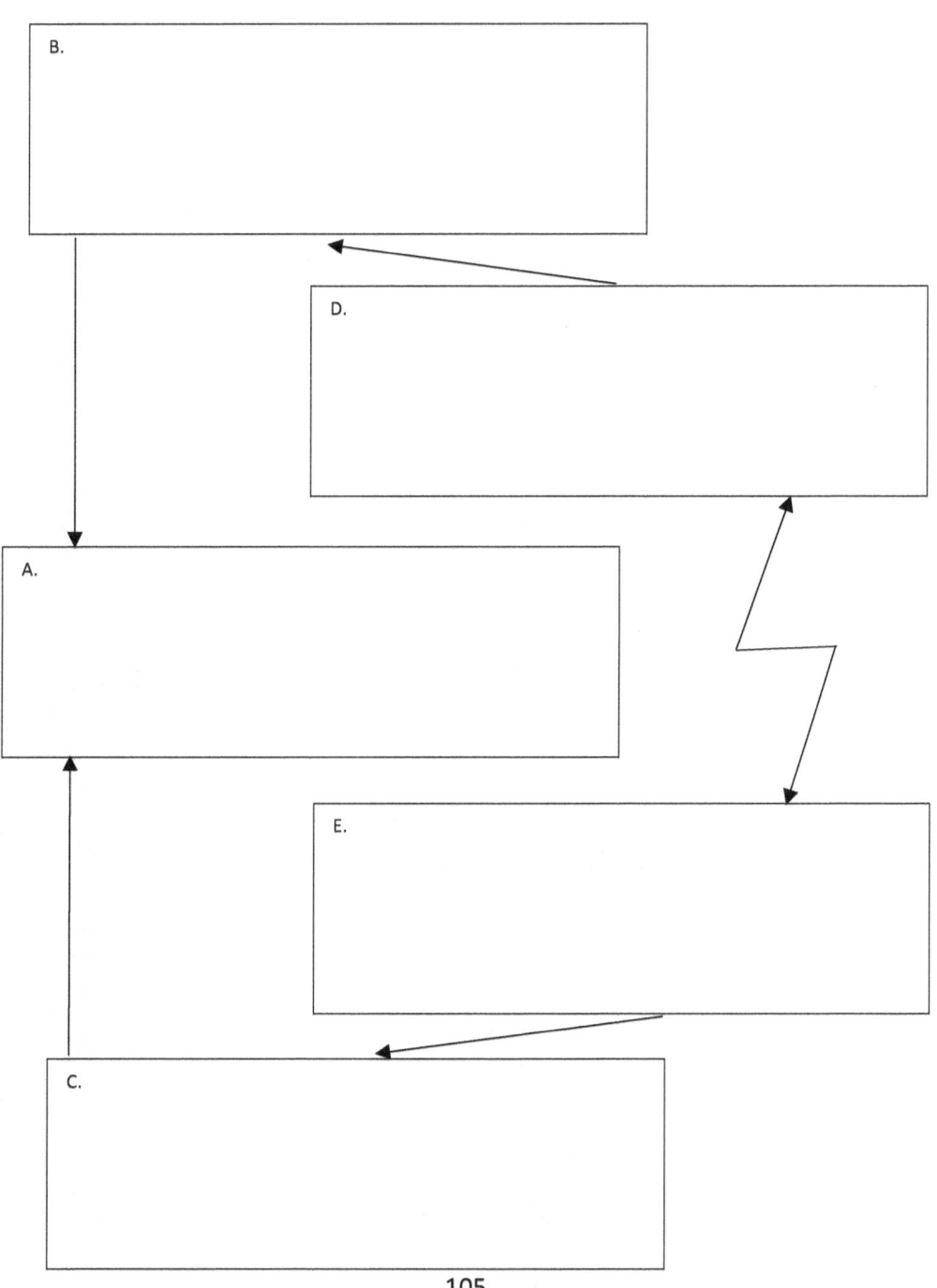

Step 5:

ABA

ACA

BDA

Silver Bullets

CEA

BEA

CDA

DEA

Step 6.

ABI

[ ]

ACI

[ ]

BDI

[ ]

Silver Bullets

CEI

BEI

CDI

DEI

Shane Ayers

Day-to-Day Conflict Worksheet 2

Step 1.

Silver Bullets

Step 2.

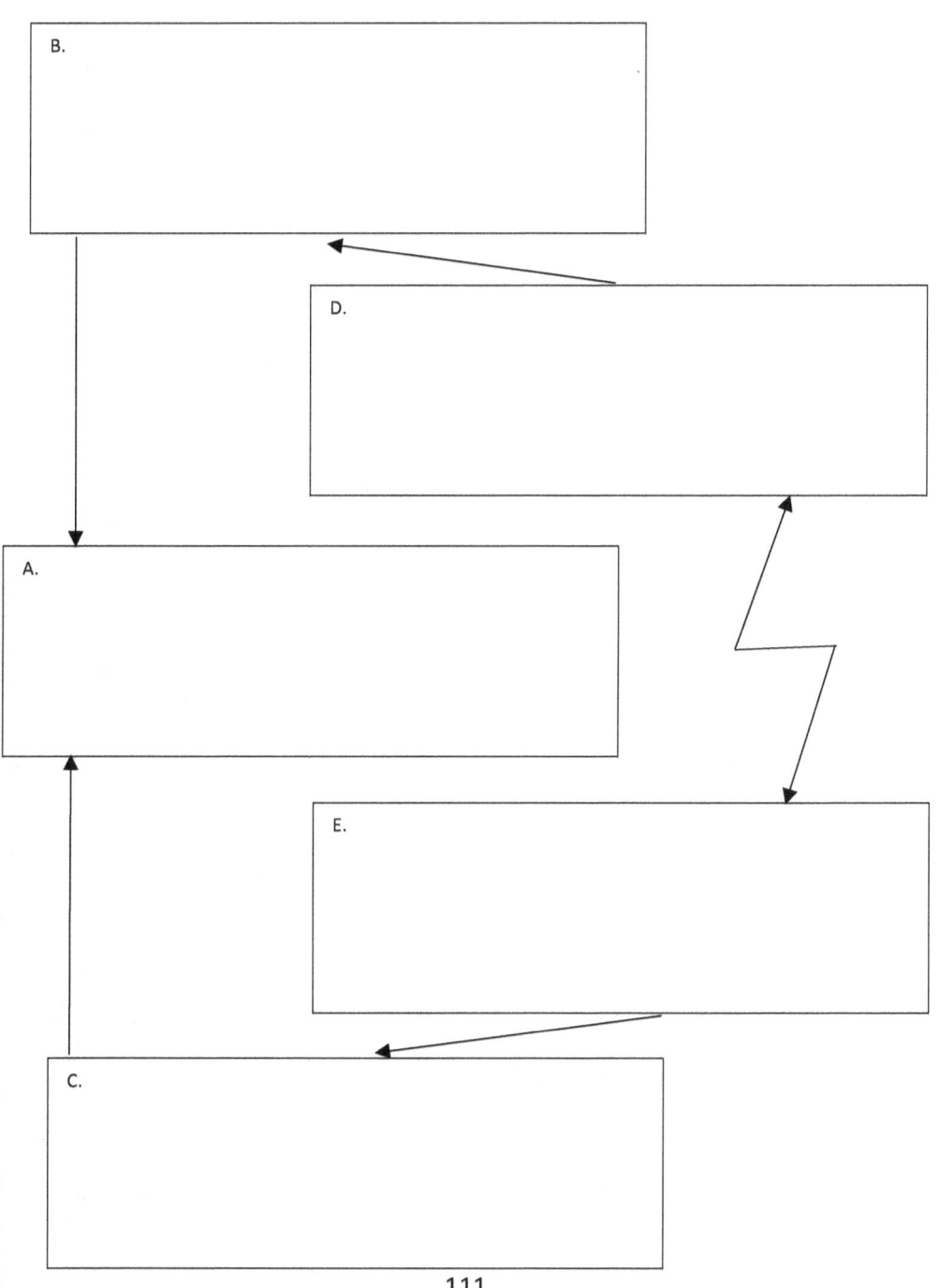

Step 4:

ABA

ACA

BDA

Silver Bullets

CEA

BEA

CDA

DEA

Step 5.

ABI

ACI

BDI

Silver Bullets

CEI

BEI

CDI

DEI

Step 6.

Use the following script to present your solution to a Day-to-Day Conflict after selecting which of the entries for Step 6 you would prefer to use.

Preferred solution for a day-to-day conflict:

| |
| |

Script: We have a difference of opinions on the issue of . . . I have been thinking about it and I would like to work with you on finding a workable solution. You want D and I want D'. These two are not compatible. I suggest we go with your D but we need to ensure that my C is taken care of as well. Do you have any suggestion how we can take care of it?

Silver Bullets

Day-to-Day Conflict Worksheet 3

Step 1.

Step 2.

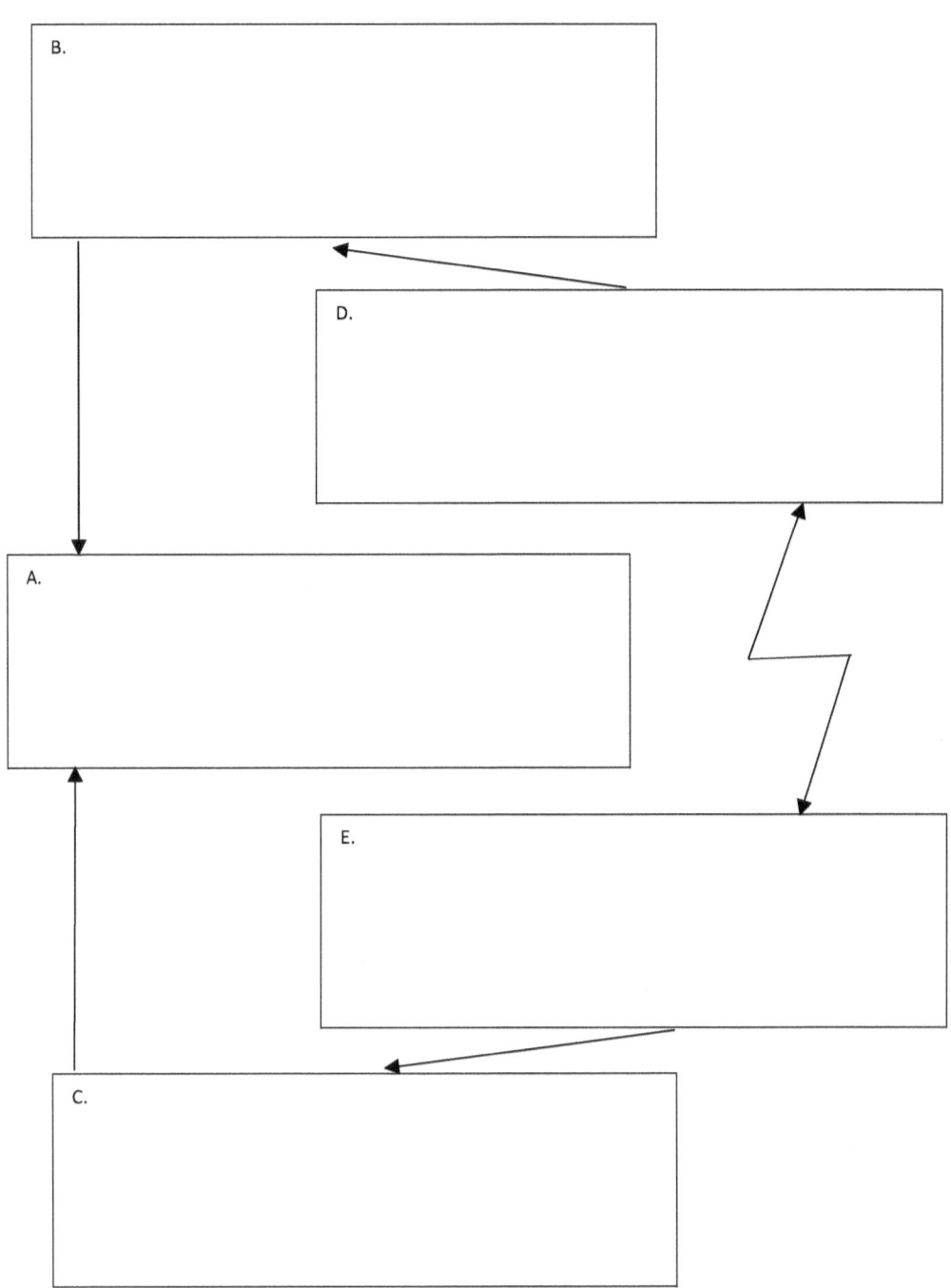

Silver Bullets

Step 4:

ABA

ACA

BDA

CEA

BEA

CDA

DEA

Silver Bullets

Step 5.

ABI

ACI

BDI

CEI

BEI

CDI

DEI

Silver Bullets

Step 6.

Use the following script to present your solution to a Day-to-Day Conflict after selecting which of the entries for Step 6 you would prefer to use.

Preferred solution for a day-to-day conflict:

Script: We have a difference of opinions on the issue of . . . I have been thinking about it and I would like to work with you on finding a workable solution. You want D and I want D'. These two are not compatible. I suggest we go with your D but we need to ensure that my C is taken care of as well. Do you have any suggestion how we can take care of it?

Shane Ayers

Day-to-Day Conflict Worksheet 4

Step 1.

Silver Bullets

Step 2.

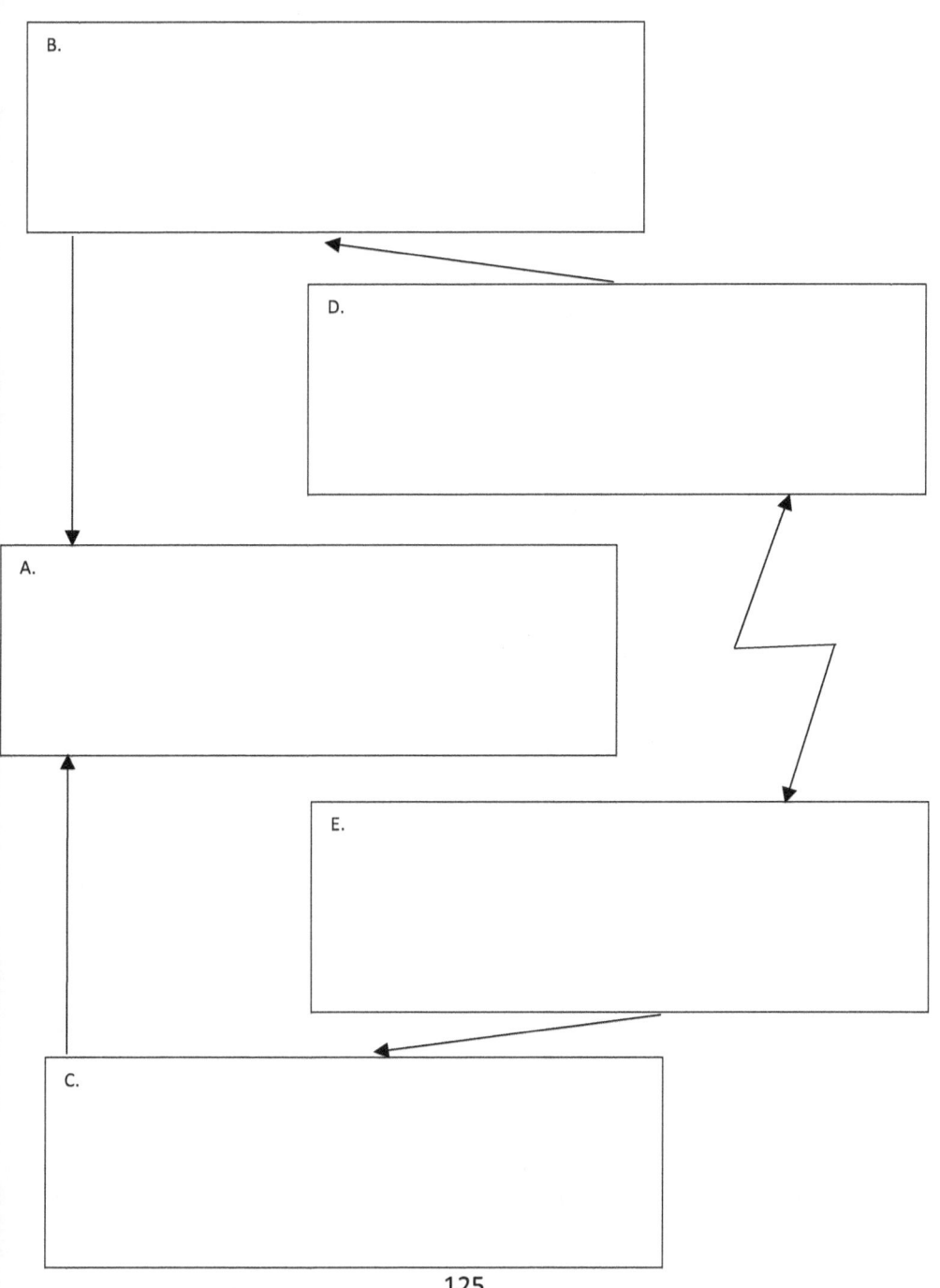

Step 4:

ABA

```
┌─────────────────────────────────────────────┐
│                                             │
│                                             │
│                                             │
│                                             │
└─────────────────────────────────────────────┘
```

ACA

```
┌─────────────────────────────────────────────┐
│                                             │
│                                             │
│                                             │
│                                             │
└─────────────────────────────────────────────┘
```

BDA

```
┌─────────────────────────────────────────────┐
│                                             │
│                                             │
│                                             │
│                                             │
└─────────────────────────────────────────────┘
```

Silver Bullets

CEA

BEA

CDA

DEA

Step 5.

ABI

ACI

BDI

Silver Bullets

CEI

BEI

CDI

DEI

Step 6.

Use the following script to present your solution to a Day-to-Day Conflict after selecting which of the entries for Step 6 you would prefer to use.

Preferred solution for a day-to-day conflict:

| |
| |
| |

Script: We have a difference of opinions on the issue of . . . I have been thinking about it and I would like to work with you on finding a workable solution. You want D and I want D'. These two are not compatible. I suggest we go with your D but we need to ensure that my C is taken care of as well. Do you have any suggestion how we can take care of it?

Silver Bullets

Day-to-Day Conflict Worksheet 5

Step 1.

Step 2.

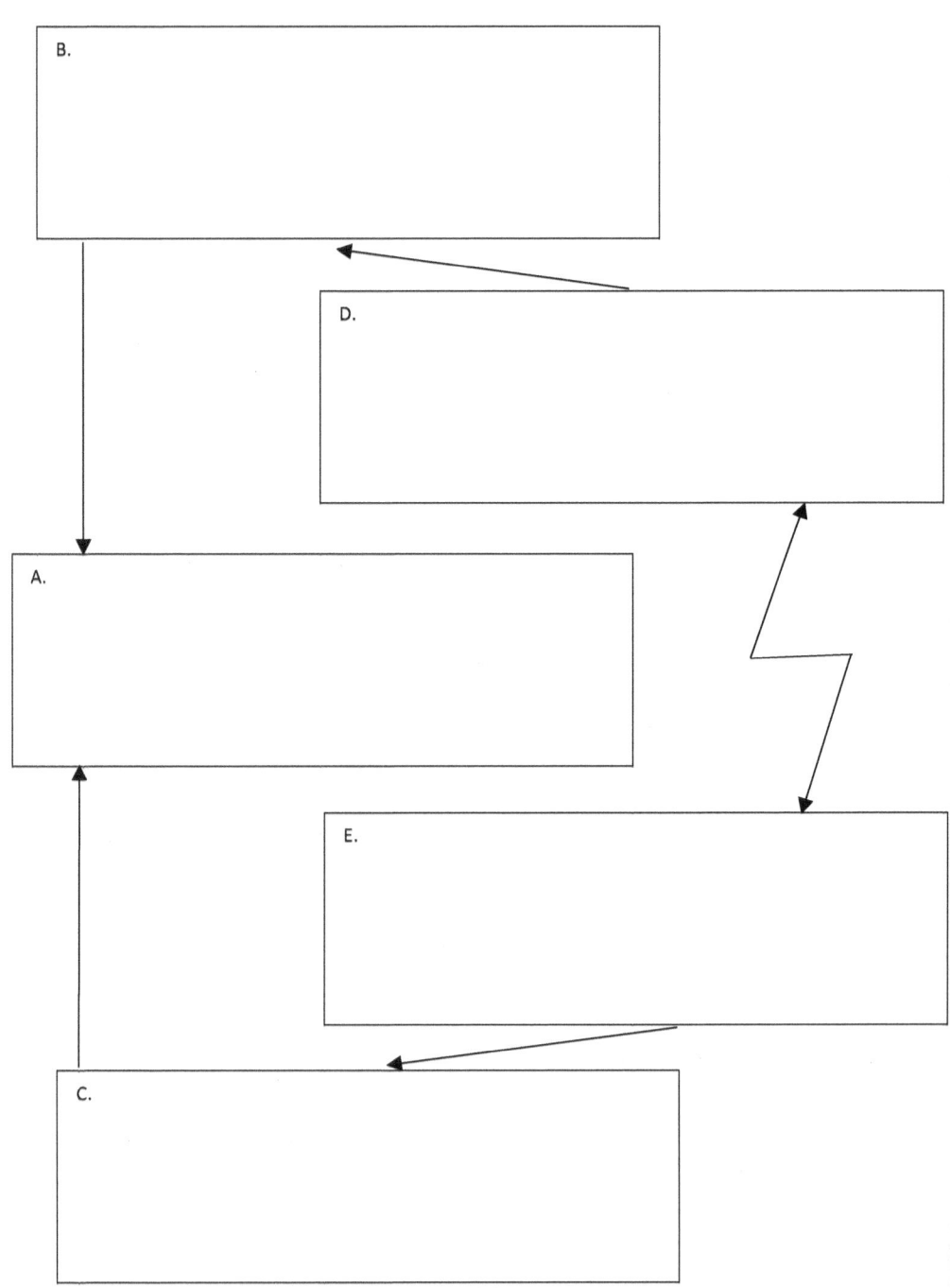

Silver Bullets

Step 4:

ABA

ACA

BDA

CEA

BEA

CDA

DEA

Silver Bullets

Step 5.

ABI

[   ]

ACI

[   ]

BDI

[   ]

CEI

BEI

CDI

DEI

Silver Bullets

Step 6.

Use the following script to present your solution to a Day-to-Day Conflict after selecting which of the entries for Step 6 you would prefer to use.

Preferred solution for a day-to-day conflict:

Script: We have a difference of opinions on the issue of . . . I have been thinking about it and I would like to work with you on finding a workable solution. You want D and I want D'. These two are not compatible. I suggest we go with your D but we need to ensure that my C is taken care of as well. Do you have any suggestion how we can take care of it?

Shane Ayers

Firefighting Situation Worksheet 2

Step 1.

Silver Bullets

Step 2.

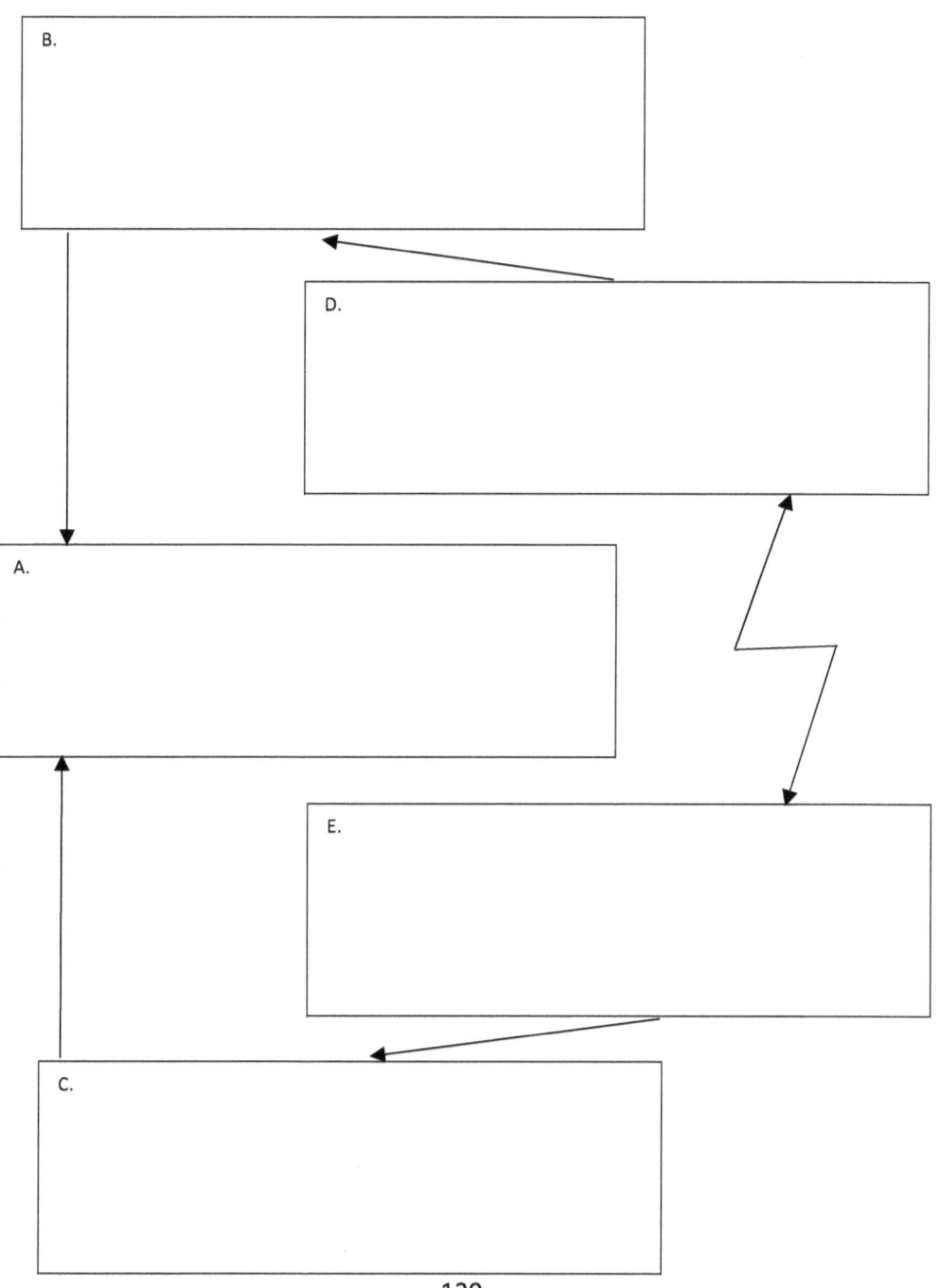

Step 4:

ABA

ACA

BDA

Silver Bullets

CEA

BEA

CDA

DEA

Step 5.

ABI

```
┌─────────────────────────────────────────┐
│                                         │
│                                         │
│                                         │
│                                         │
└─────────────────────────────────────────┘
```

ACI

```
┌─────────────────────────────────────────┐
│                                         │
│                                         │
│                                         │
│                                         │
└─────────────────────────────────────────┘
```

BDI

```
┌─────────────────────────────────────────┐
│                                         │
│                                         │
│                                         │
│                                         │
└─────────────────────────────────────────┘
```

Silver Bullets

CEI

BEI

CDI

DEI

Combined solution for a firefighting conflict:

[ ]

A

[ ]

B

[ ]

C

[ ]

D

[ ]

E

[ ]

Silver Bullets

Notes from person who raised the problem:

Alternate solution from person who raised the problem:

Silver Bullets

Notes from the key person associated with the procedure:

Alternate solution from the key person associated with the procedure:

Silver Bullets

Firefighting Situation Worksheet 3

Step 1.

Step 3.

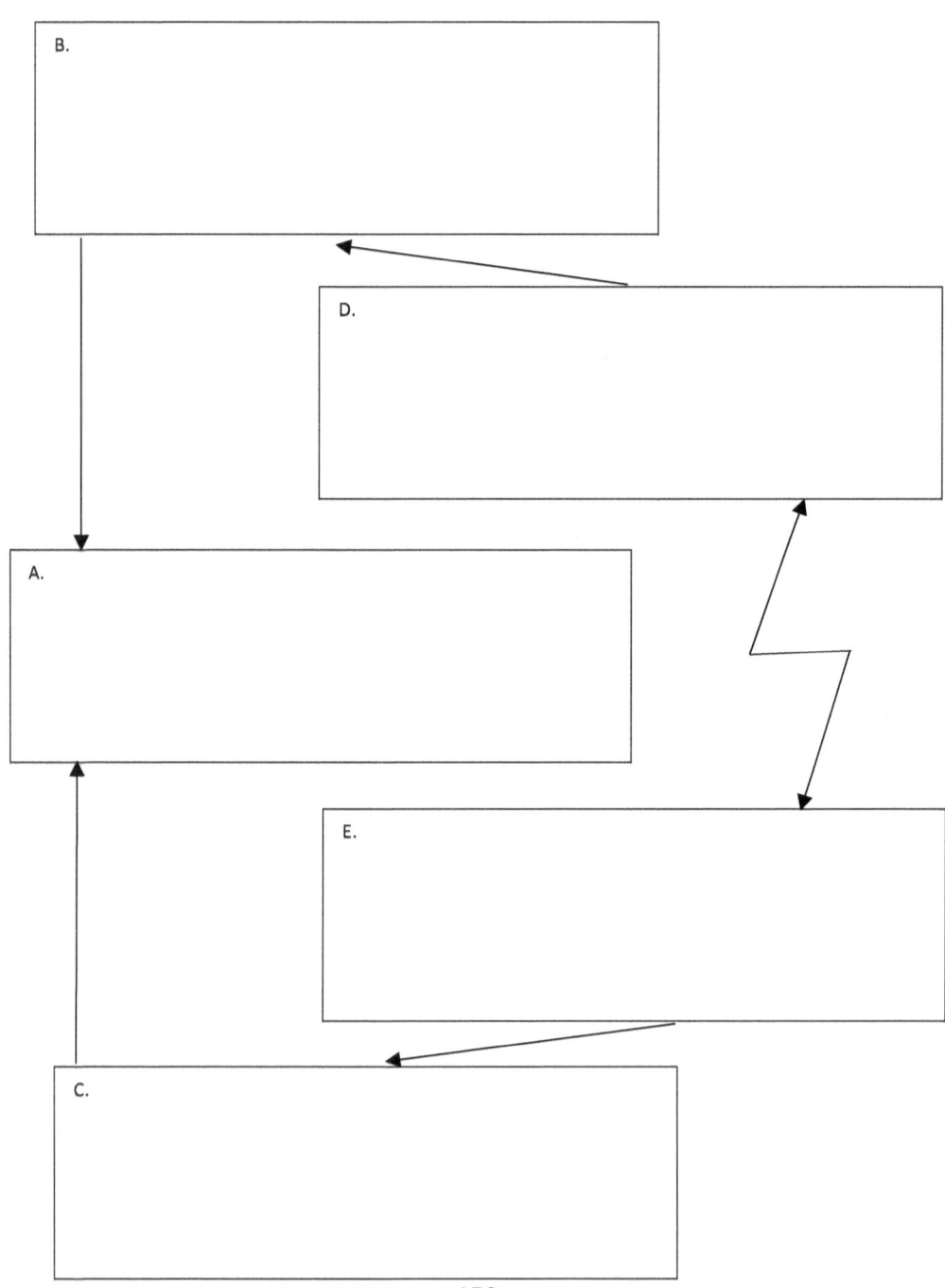

Silver Bullets

Step 5:

ABA

ACA

BDA

CEA

BEA

CDA

DEA

Silver Bullets

Step 6.

ABI

ACI

BDI

CEI

BEI

CDI

DEI

Silver Bullets

Combined solution for a firefighting conflict:

A

B

C

D

E

Notes from person who raised the problem:

Silver Bullets

Alternate solution from person who raised the problem:

Notes from the key person associated with the procedure:

Silver Bullets

Alternate solution from the key person associated with the procedure:

Shane Ayers

Firefighting Situation Worksheet 4

Step 1.

Silver Bullets

Step 2.

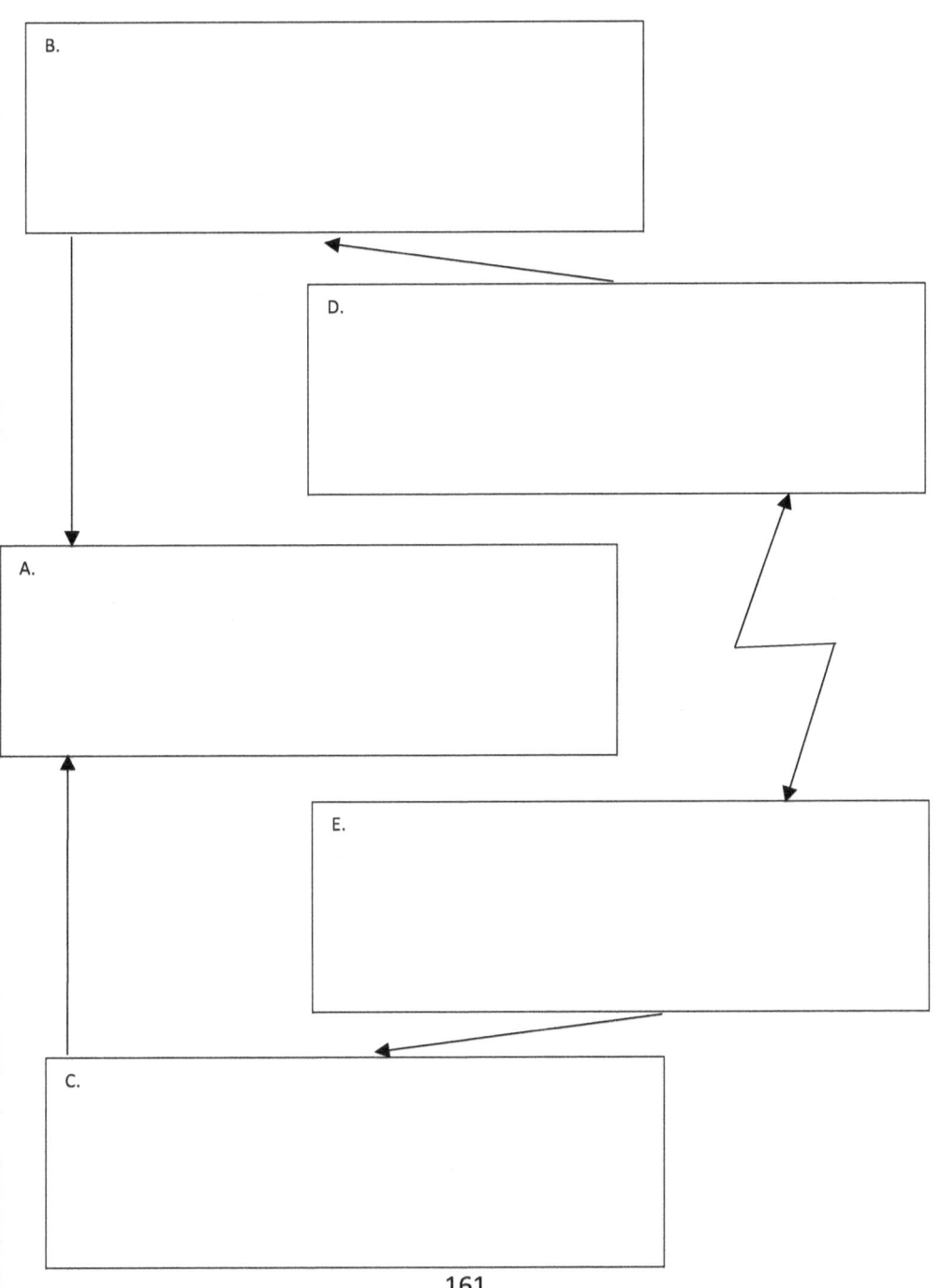

Step 5:

ABA

ACA

BDA

Silver Bullets

CEA

BEA

CDA

DEA

Step 6.

ABI

ACI

BDI

Silver Bullets

CEI

BEI

CDI

DEI

Shane Ayers

Combined solution for a firefighting conflict:

A

B

C

D

E

Silver Bullets

Notes from person who raised the problem:

Alternate solution from person who raised the problem:

Silver Bullets

Notes from the key person associated with the procedure:

Alternate solution from the key person associated with the procedure:

Silver Bullets

Firefighting Situation Worksheet 5

Step 1.

Step 3.

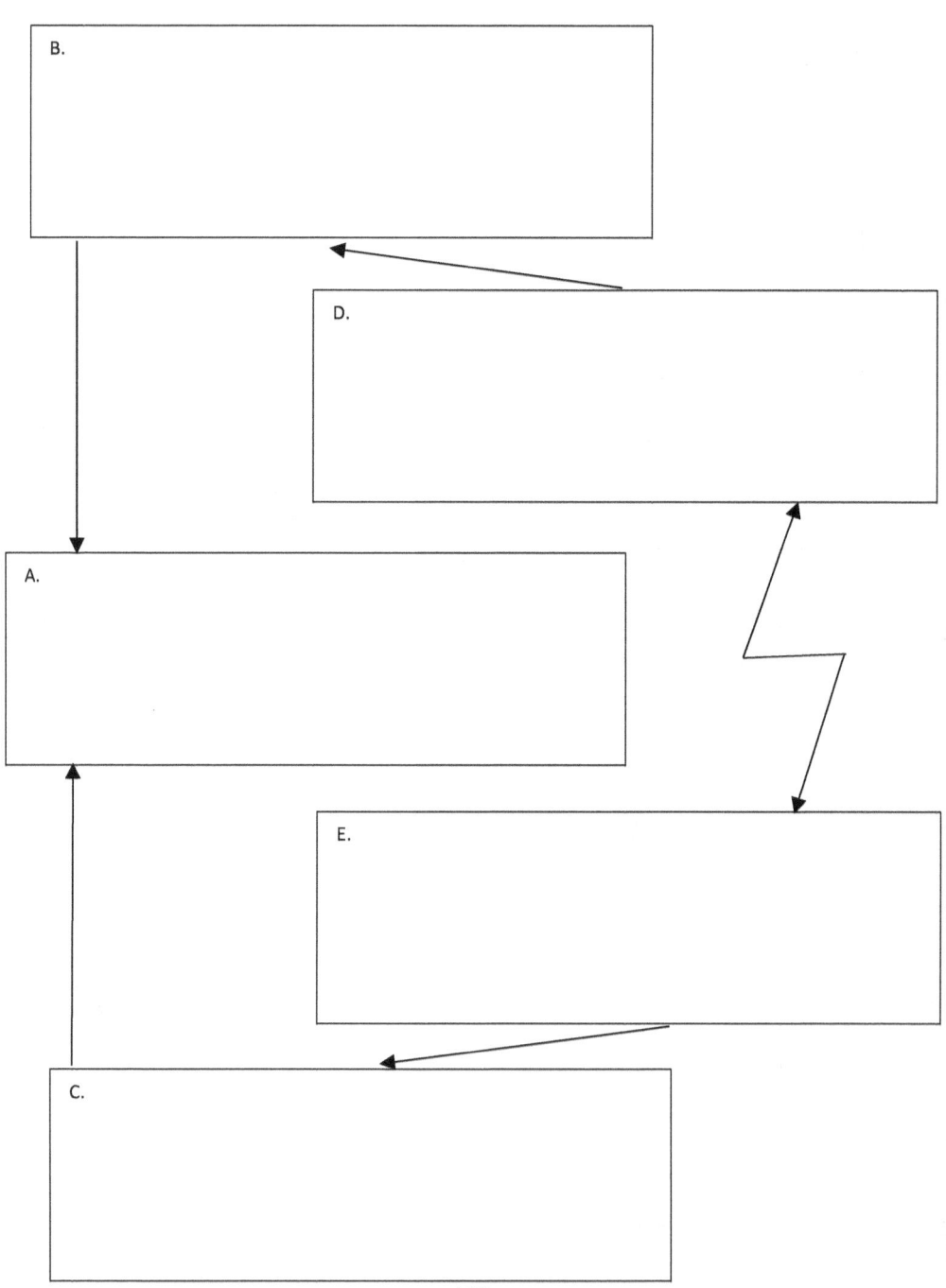

Silver Bullets

Step 5:

ABA

ACA

BDA

CEA

BEA

CDA

DEA

Silver Bullets

Step 6.

ABI

ACI

BDI

CEI

BEI

CDI

DEI

Silver Bullets

Combined solution for a firefighting conflict:

A

B

C

D

E

Shane Ayers

Notes from person who raised the problem:

Silver Bullets

Alternate solution from person who raised the problem:

Notes from the key person associated with the procedure:

Silver Bullets

Alternate solution from the key person associated with the procedure:

Undesirable Effects Worksheet 2
Step 1.

Step 3.

Silver Bullets

Step 4.

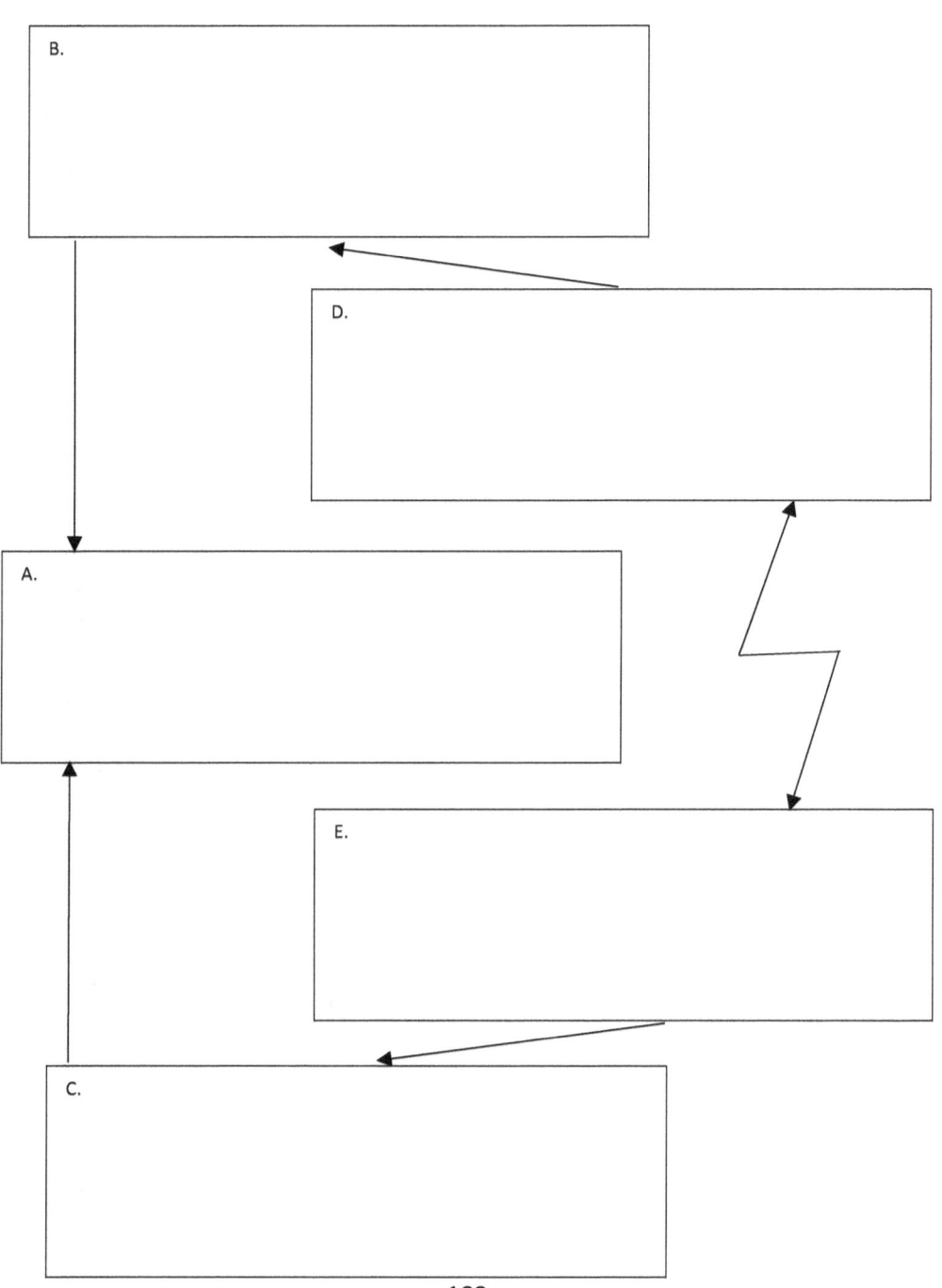

Step 6:

ABA

ACA

BDA

Silver Bullets

CEA

BEA

CDA

DEA

Step 7.

ABI

ACI

BDI

Silver Bullets

CEI

BEI

CDI

DEI

Step 8

A

B

C

D

E

Silver Bullets

Undesirable Effects Worksheet 3
Step 1.

Step 3.

Step 4.

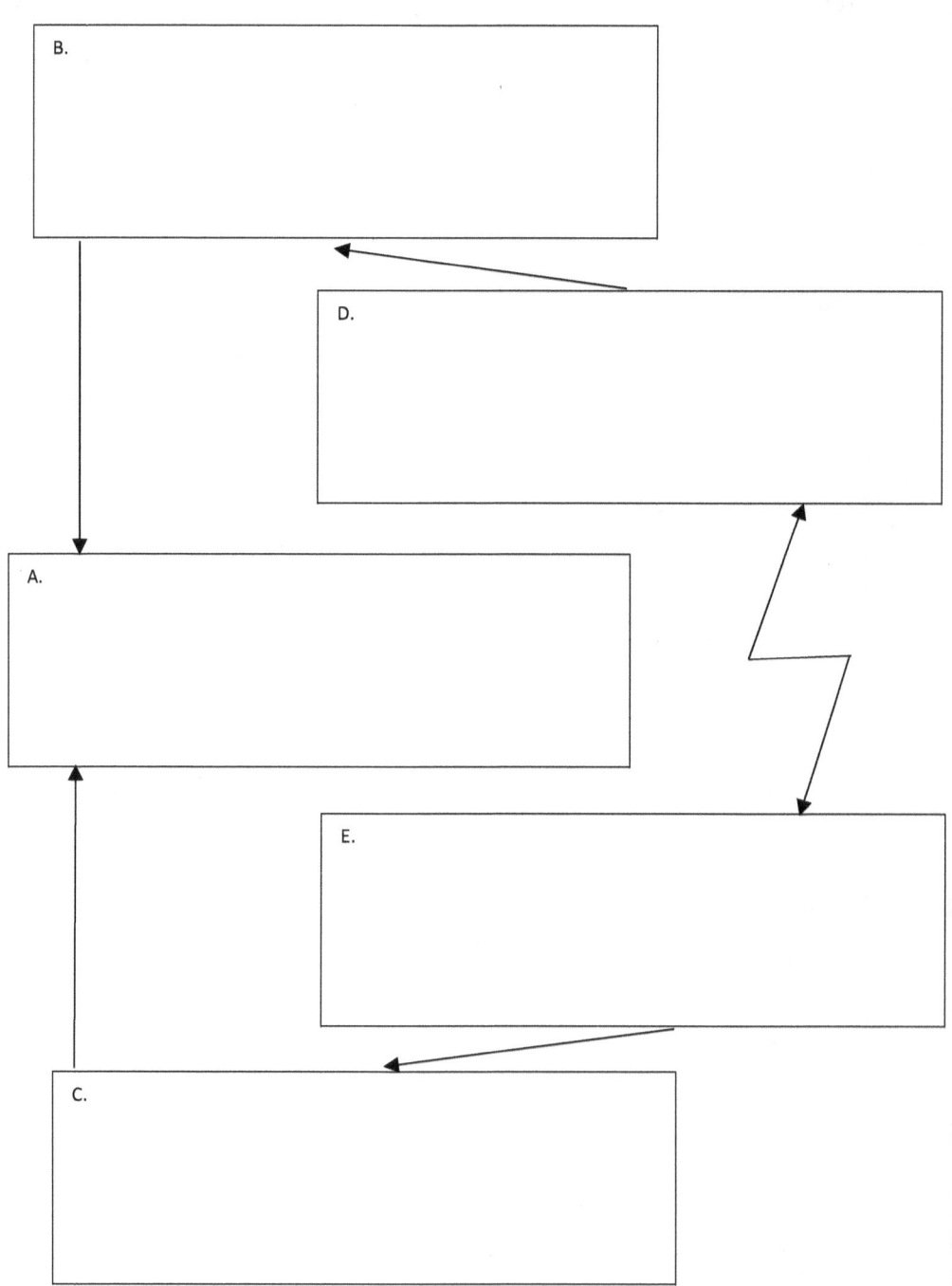

Silver Bullets

Step 6:

ABA

ACA

BDA

CEA

BEA

CDA

DEA

Silver Bullets

Step 7.

ABI

ACI

BDI

CEI

BEI

CDI

DEI

Silver Bullets

Step 8

A

B

C

D

E

Shane Ayers

Undesirable Effects Worksheet 4

Step 1.

Step 3.

Silver Bullets

Step 4.

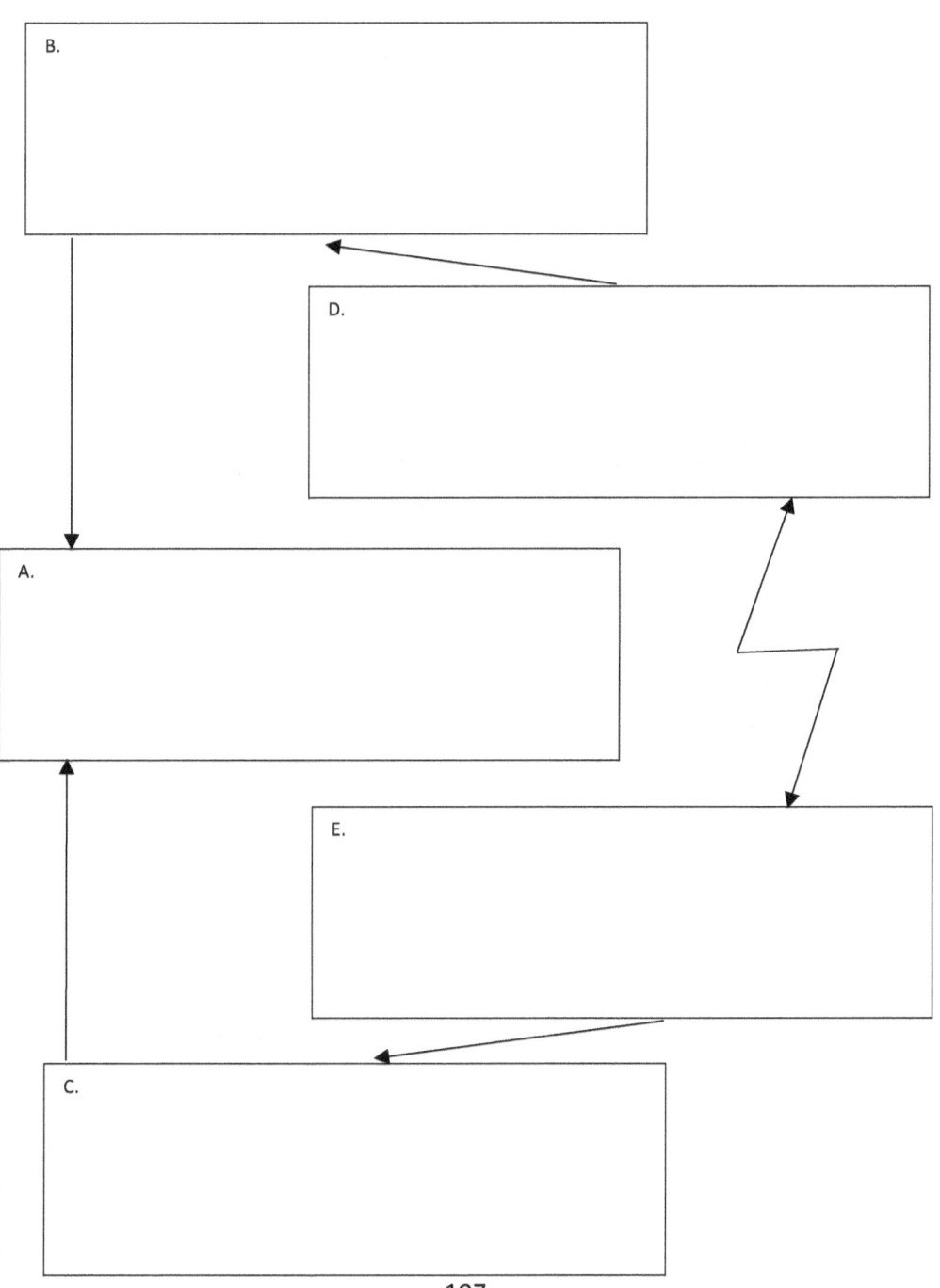

Step 6:

ABA

ACA

BDA

Silver Bullets

CEA

BEA

CDA

DEA

Step 7.

ABI

ACI

BDI

Silver Bullets

CEI

BEI

CDI

DEI

Step 8

A

B

C

D

E

Silver Bullets

Undesirable Effects Worksheet 5
Step 1.

Step 3.

Step 4.

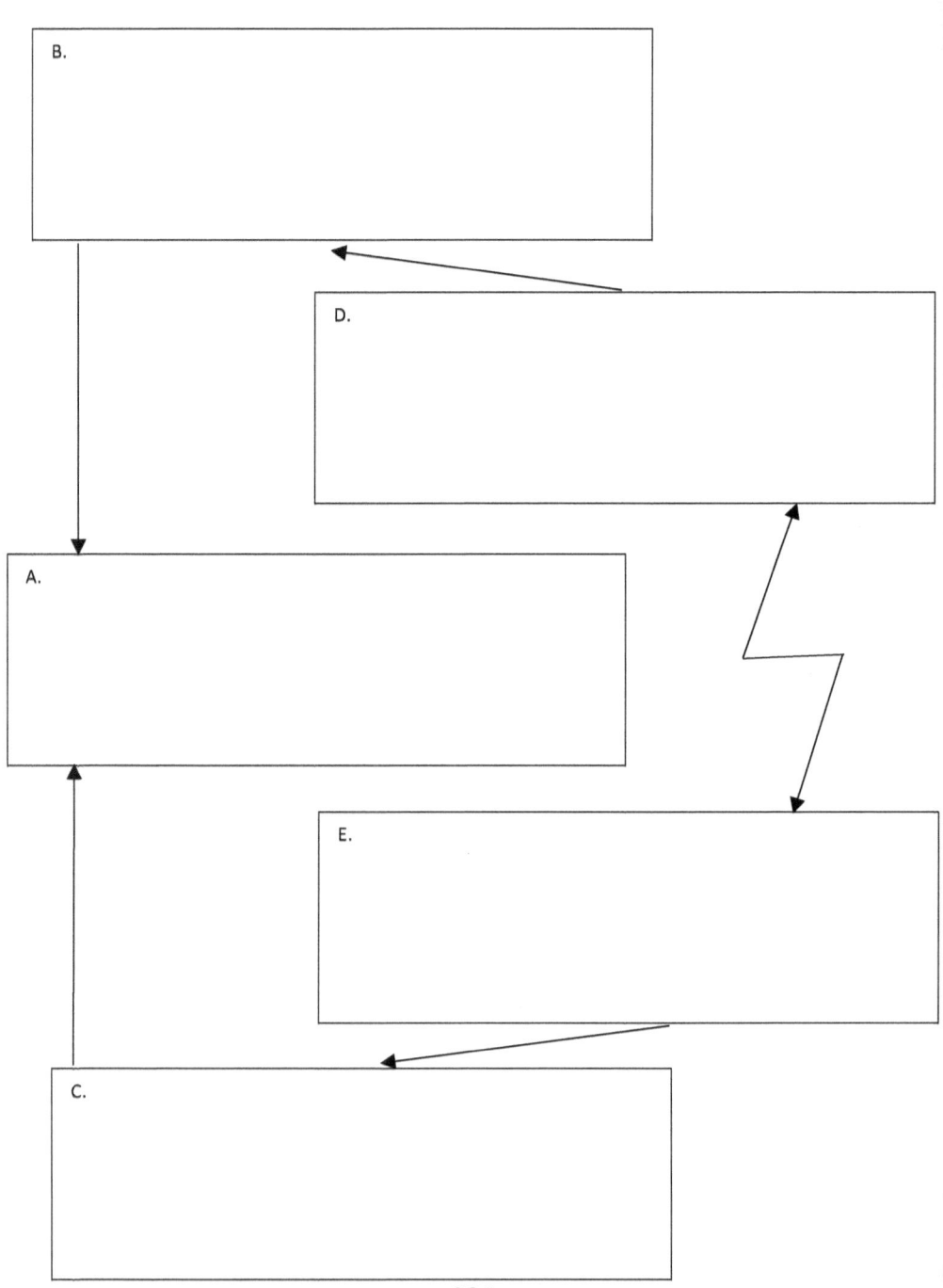

Silver Bullets

Step 6:

ABA

ACA

BDA

CEA

BEA

CDA

DEA

Silver Bullets

Step 7.

ABI

ACI

BDI

CEI

BEI

CDI

DEI

Silver Bullets

Step 8

A

B

C

D

E

Three-Cloud Approach Worksheet 2
Step 1.

Undesirable Effect 1

Undesirable Effect 2

Undesirable Effect 3

Silver Bullets

Step 3a.

Step 4a.

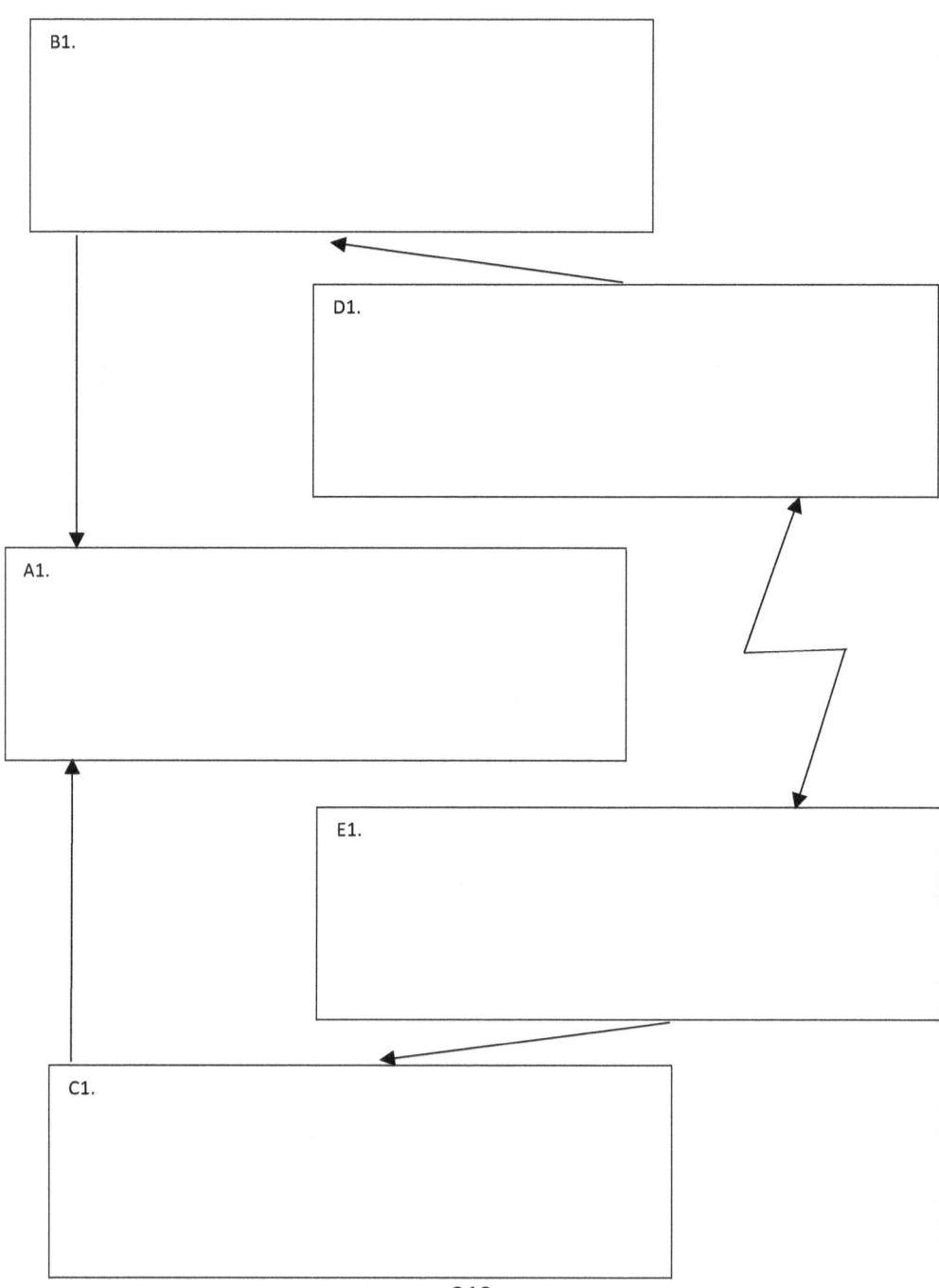

Silver Bullets

Step 6a:

ABA1

ACA1

BDA1

CEA1

BEA1

CDA1

DEA1

Silver Bullets

Step 3b.

Step 4b.

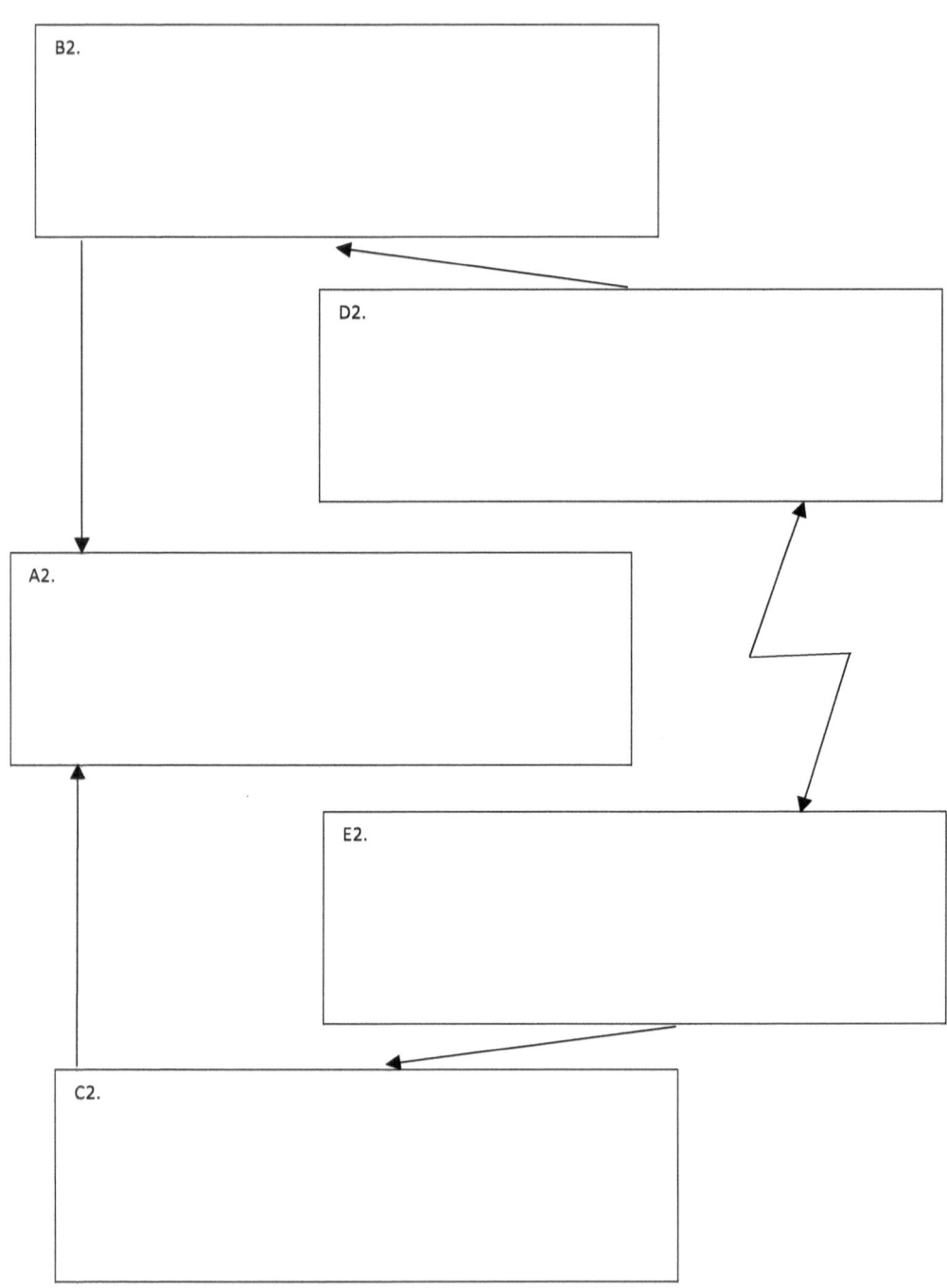

Silver Bullets

Step 6b:

ABA2

ACA2

BDA2

CEA2

BEA2

CDA2

DEA2

Silver Bullets

Step 3c.

Step 4c.

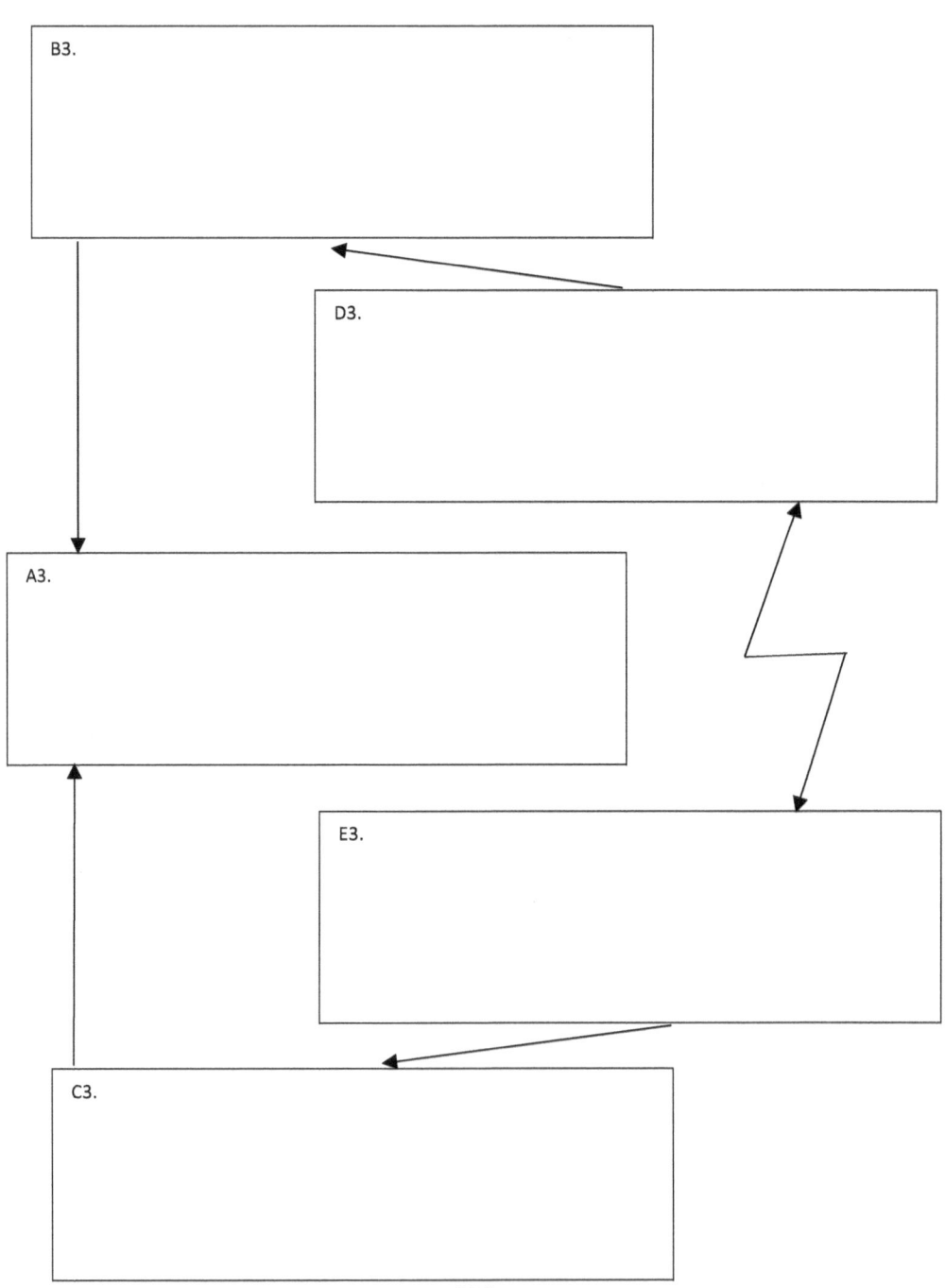

Silver Bullets

Step 6a:

ABA3

ACA3

BDA3

CEA3

BEA3

CDA3

DEA3

Silver Bullets

Step 7.

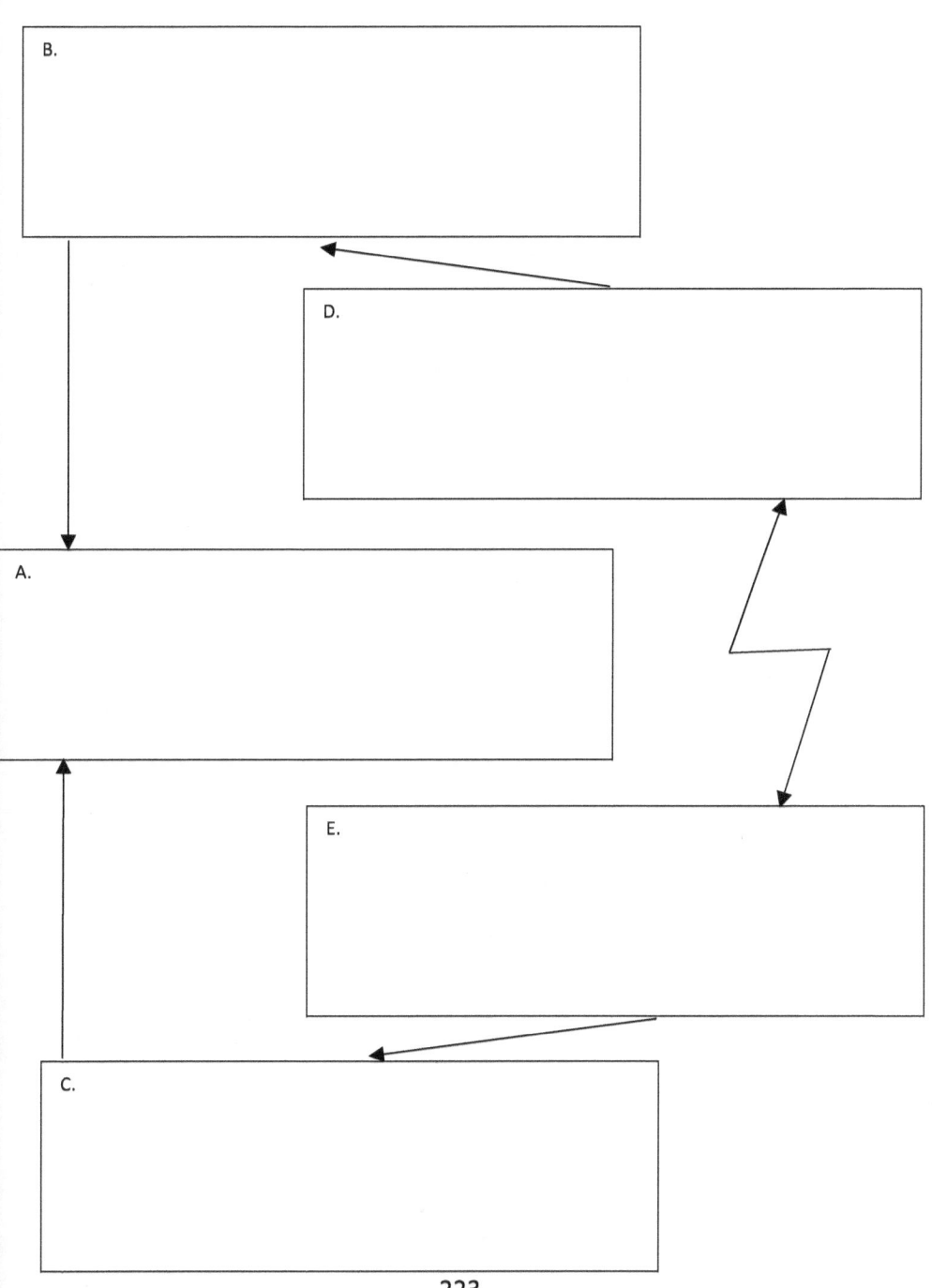

Step 8:

Generic ABA

Generic ACA

Generic BDA

Silver Bullets

Generic CEA

Generic BEA

Generic CDA

Generic DEA

Step 9.

Generic ABI

Generic ACI

Generic BDI

Silver Bullets

Generic CEI

Generic BEI

Generic CDI

Generic DEI

Step 10a.

Adapted ABI for UDE 1

Adapted ACI for UDE 1

Adapted BDI for UDE 1

Adapted CEI for UDE 1

Silver Bullets

Adapted BEI for UDE 1

Adapted CDI for UDE 1

Adapted DEI for UDE 1

Step 10a.

Adapted ABI for UDE 2

Adapted ACI for UDE 2

Adapted BDI for UDE 2

Adapted CEI for UDE 2

Silver Bullets

Adapted BEI for UDE 2

Adapted CDI for UDE 2

Adapted DEI for UDE 2

Step 10a.

Adapted ABI for UDE 3

Adapted ACI for UDE 3

Adapted BDI for UDE 3

Adapted CEI for UDE 3

Silver Bullets

Three-Cloud Approach Worksheet 3
Step 1.

Undesirable Effect 1

Undesirable Effect 2

Undesirable Effect 3

Step 3a.

Silver Bullets

Step 4a.

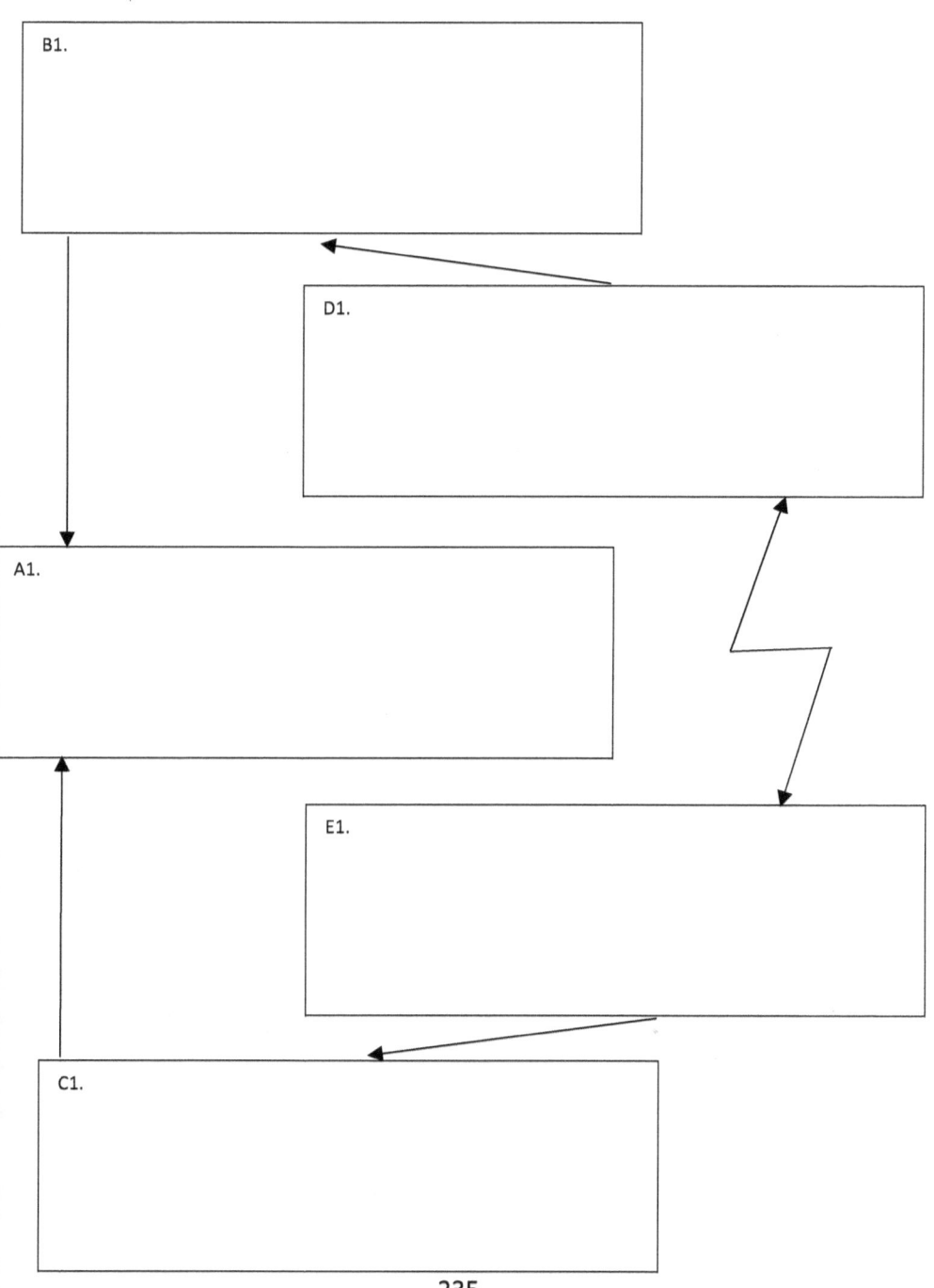

Step 6a:

ABA1

ACA1

BDA1

Silver Bullets

CEA1

BEA1

CDA1

DEA1

Step 3b.

Silver Bullets

Step 4b.

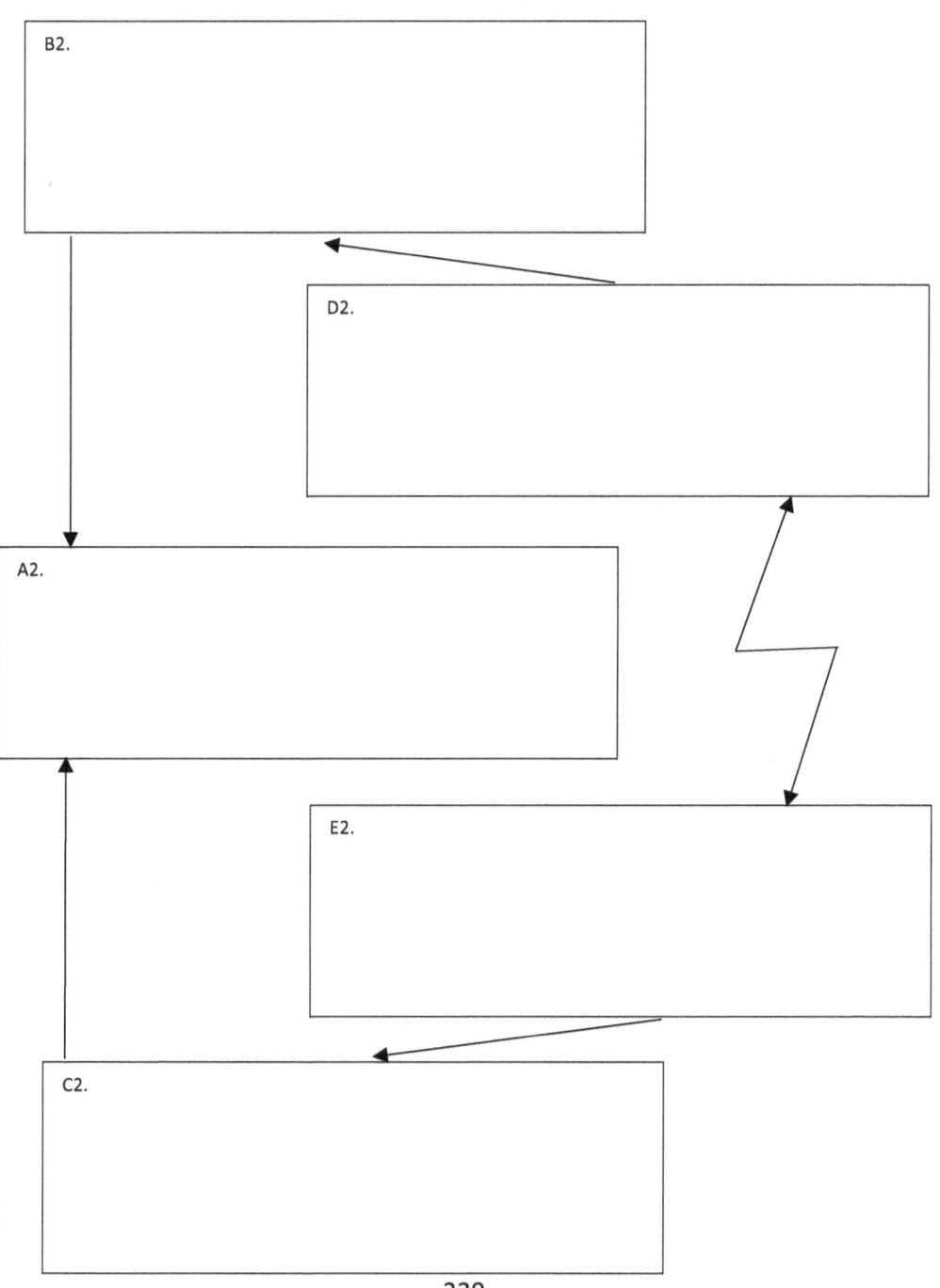

Step 6b:

ABA2

ACA2

BDA2

Silver Bullets

CEA2

BEA2

CDA2

DEA2

Step 3c.

Silver Bullets

Step 4c.

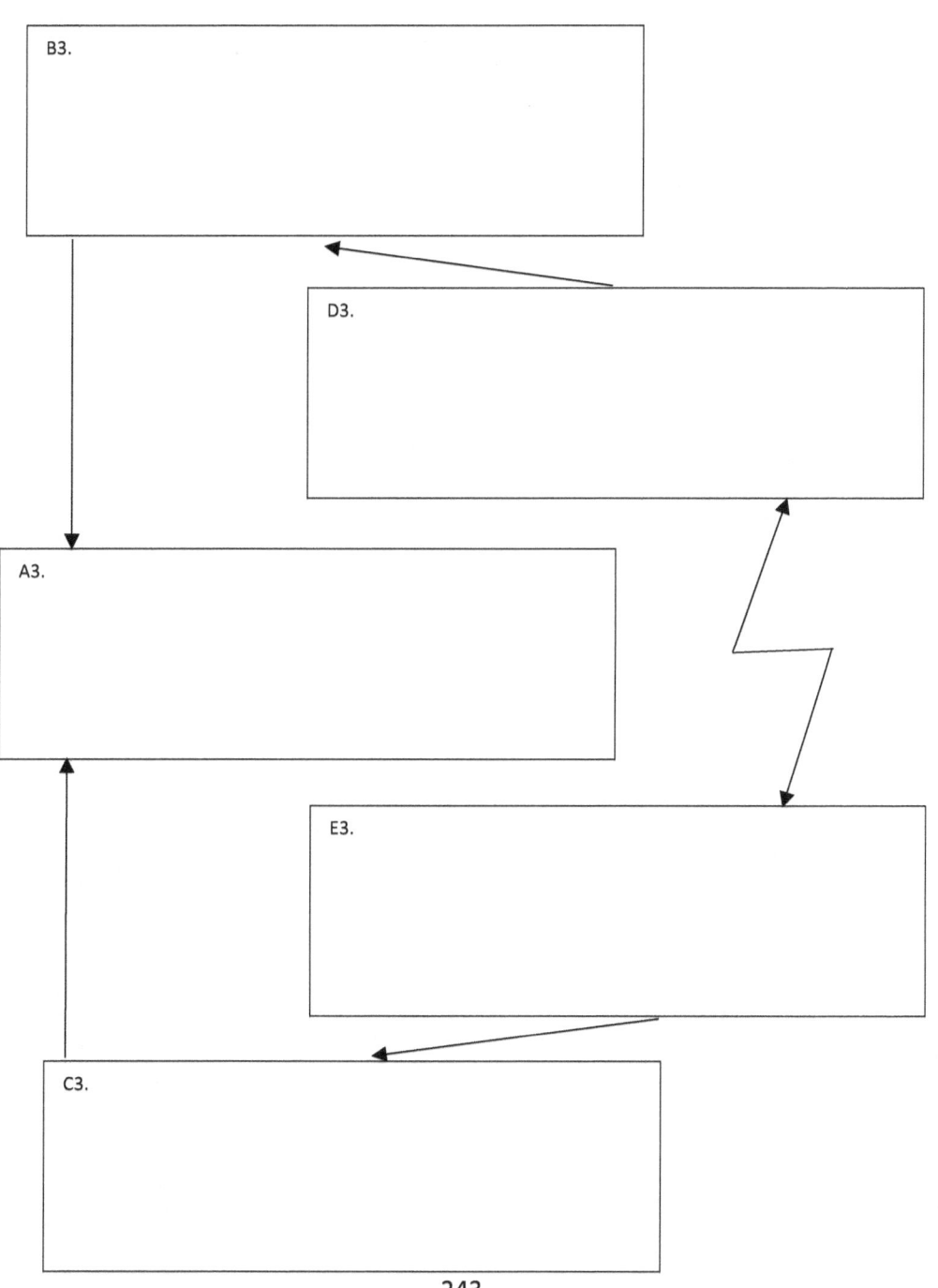

Step 6a:

ABA3

ACA3

BDA3

Silver Bullets

CEA3

BEA3

CDA3

DEA3

Step 7.

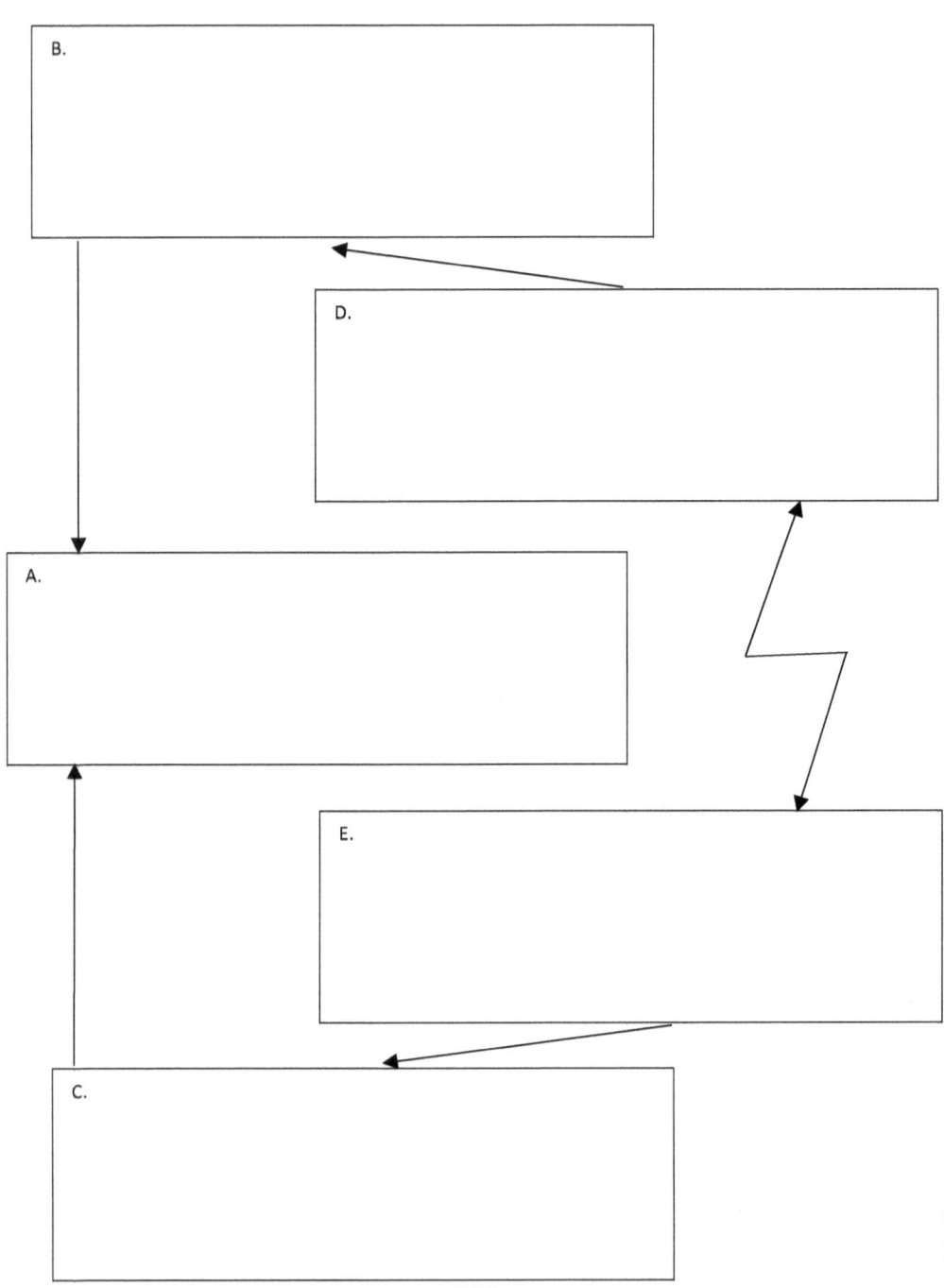

Silver Bullets

Step 8:

Generic ABA

Generic ACA

Generic BDA

Generic CEA

Generic BEA

Generic CDA

Generic DEA

Silver Bullets

Step 9.

Generic ABI

Generic ACI

Generic BDI

Generic CEI

Generic BEI

Generic CDI

Generic DEI

Silver Bullets

Step 10a.

Adapted ABI for UDE 1

Adapted ACI for UDE 1

Adapted BDI for UDE 1

Adapted CEI for UDE 1

Adapted BEI for UDE 1

Adapted CDI for UDE 1

Adapted DEI for UDE 1

Silver Bullets

Step 10a.

Adapted ABI for UDE 2

Adapted ACI for UDE 2

Adapted BDI for UDE 2

Adapted CEI for UDE 2

Adapted BEI for UDE 2

Adapted CDI for UDE 2

Adapted DEI for UDE 2

Silver Bullets

Step 10a.

Adapted ABI for UDE 3

Adapted ACI for UDE 3

Adapted BDI for UDE 3

Adapted CEI for UDE 3

Shane Ayers

Three-Cloud Approach Worksheet 4
Step 1.

Undesirable Effect 1

Undesirable Effect 2

Undesirable Effect 3

Silver Bullets

Step 3a.

Step 4a.

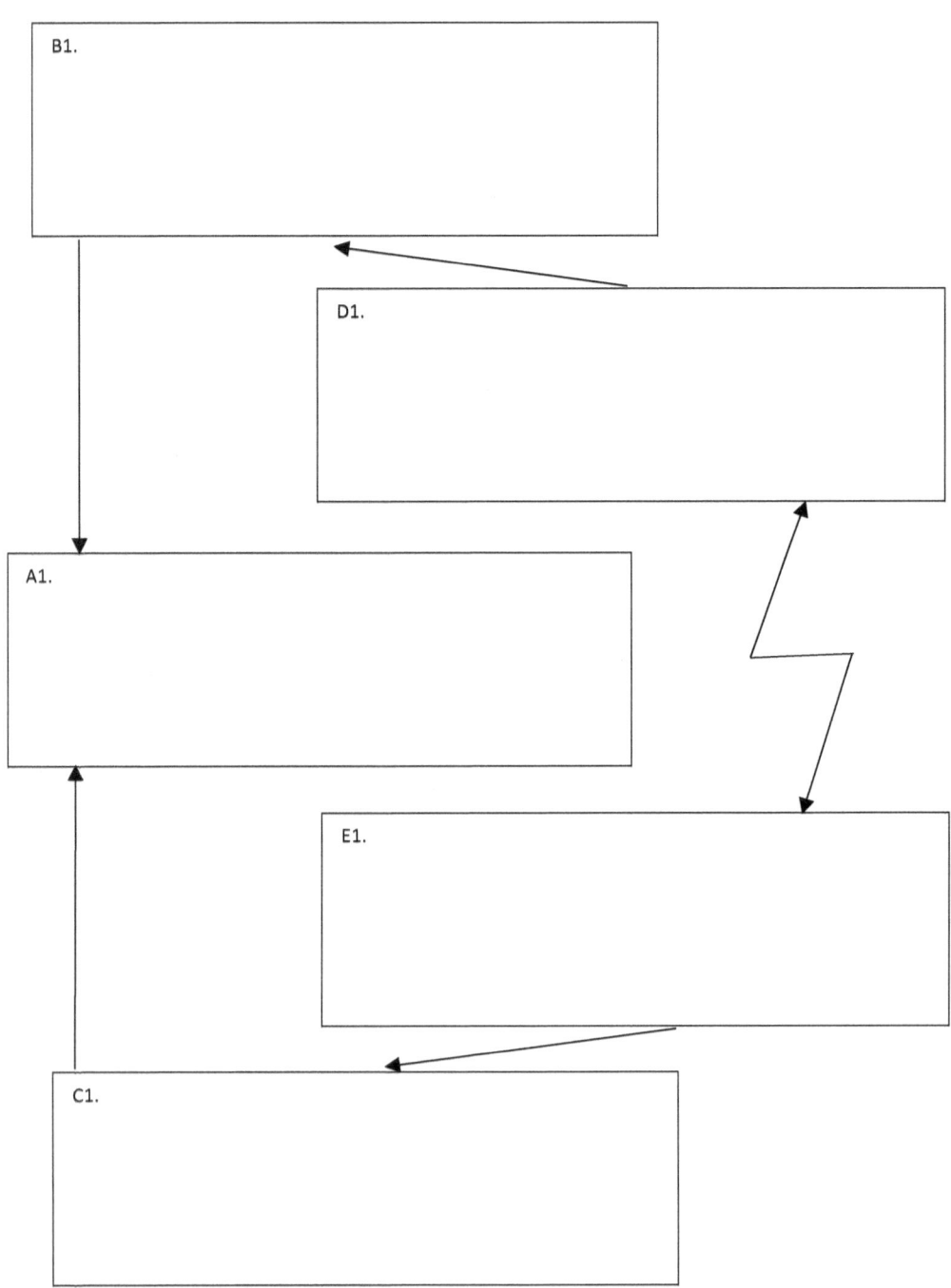

Silver Bullets

Step 6a:

ABA1

ACA1

BDA1

CEA1

BEA1

CDA1

DEA1

Silver Bullets

Step 3b.

Step 4b.

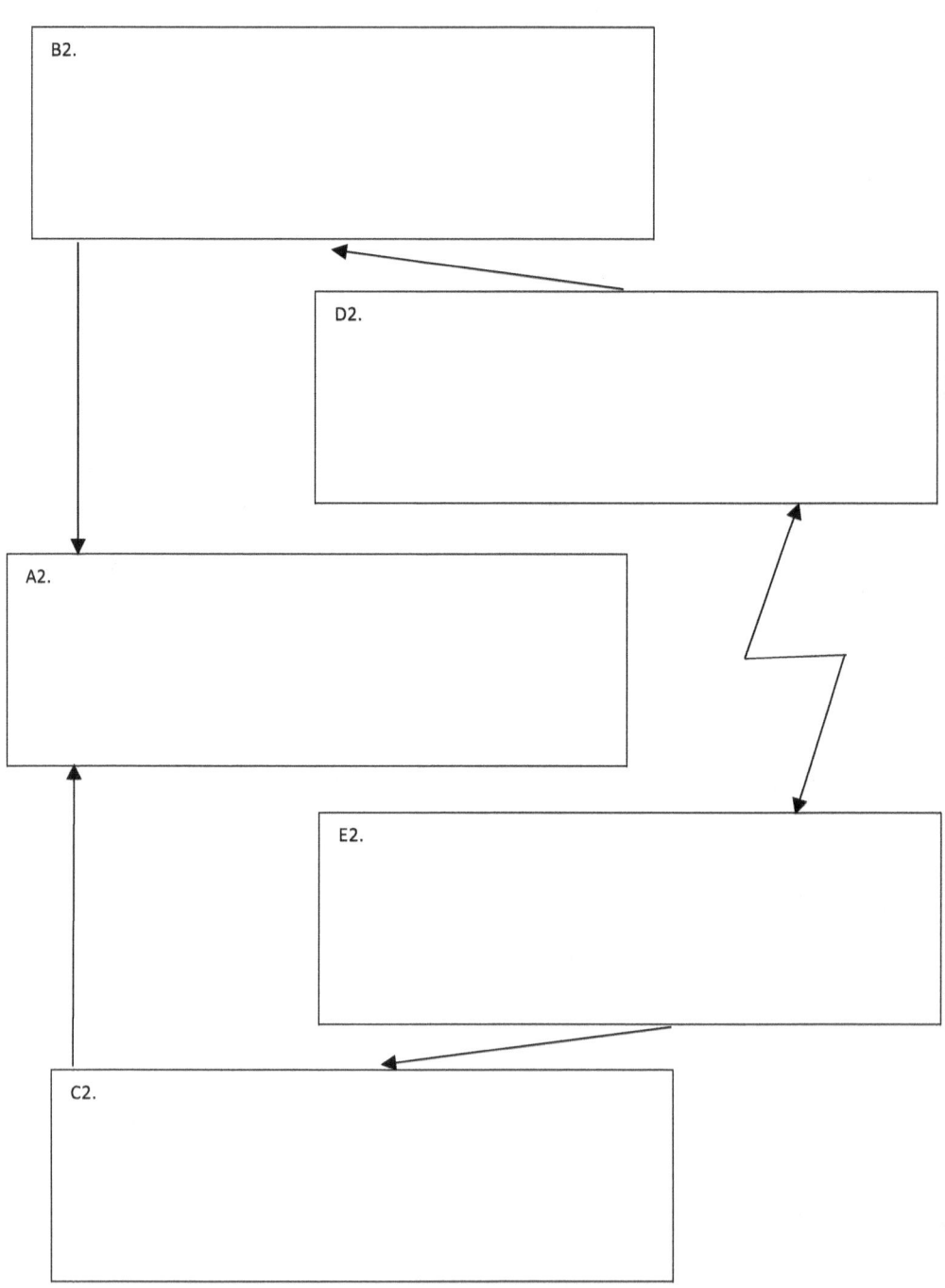

Silver Bullets

Step 6b:

ABA2

ACA2

BDA2

CEA2

BEA2

CDA2

DEA2

Silver Bullets

Step 3c.

Step 4c.

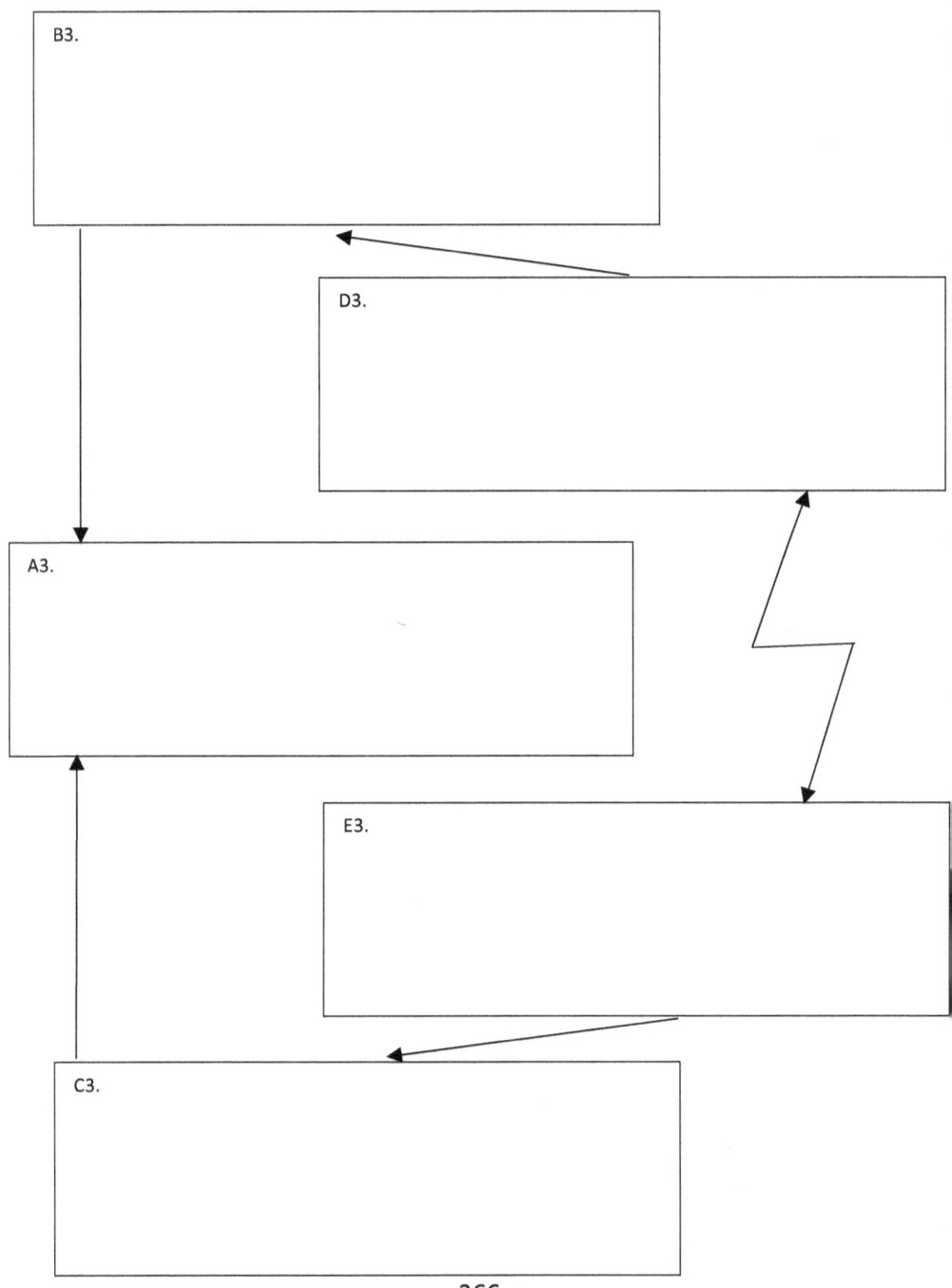

Silver Bullets

Step 6a:

ABA3

ACA3

BDA3

CEA3

BEA3

CDA3

DEA3

Silver Bullets

Step 7.

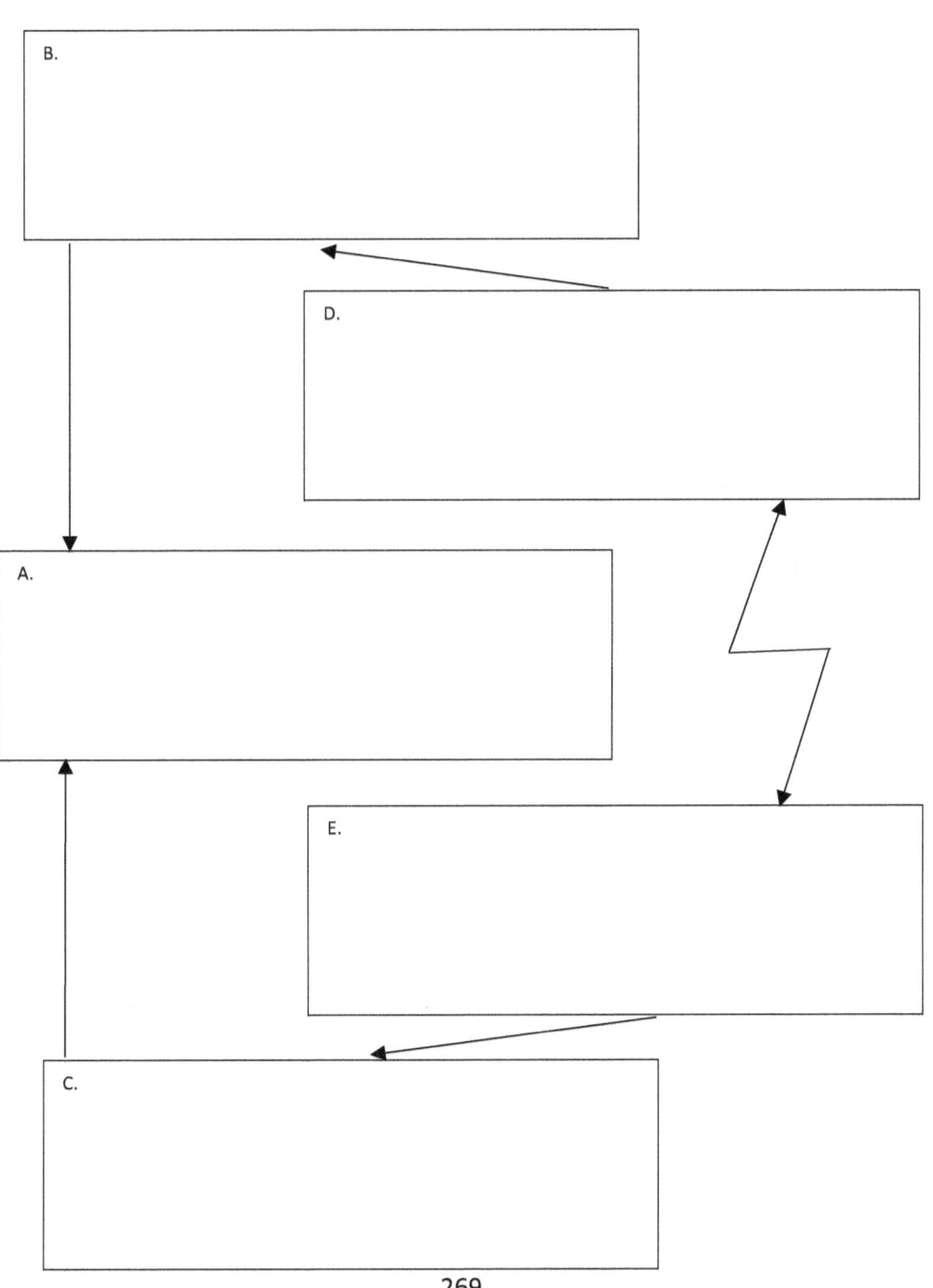

Step 8:

Generic ABA

Generic ACA

Generic BDA

Silver Bullets

Generic CEA

Generic BEA

Generic CDA

Generic DEA

Step 9.

Generic ABI

Generic ACI

Generic BDI

Silver Bullets

Generic CEI

Generic BEI

Generic CDI

Generic DEI

Step 10a.

Adapted ABI for UDE 1

Adapted ACI for UDE 1

Adapted BDI for UDE 1

Adapted CEI for UDE 1

Silver Bullets

Adapted BEI for UDE 1

Adapted CDI for UDE 1

Adapted DEI for UDE 1

Step 10a.

Adapted ABI for UDE 2

Adapted ACI for UDE 2

Adapted BDI for UDE 2

Adapted CEI for UDE 2

Silver Bullets

Adapted BEI for UDE 2

Adapted CDI for UDE 2

Adapted DEI for UDE 2

Step 10a.

Adapted ABI for UDE 3

Adapted ACI for UDE 3

Adapted BDI for UDE 3

Adapted CEI for UDE 3

Silver Bullets

Three-Cloud Approach Worksheet 5
Step 1.

Undesirable Effect 1

Undesirable Effect 2

Undesirable Effect 3

Step 3a.

Silver Bullets

Step 4a.

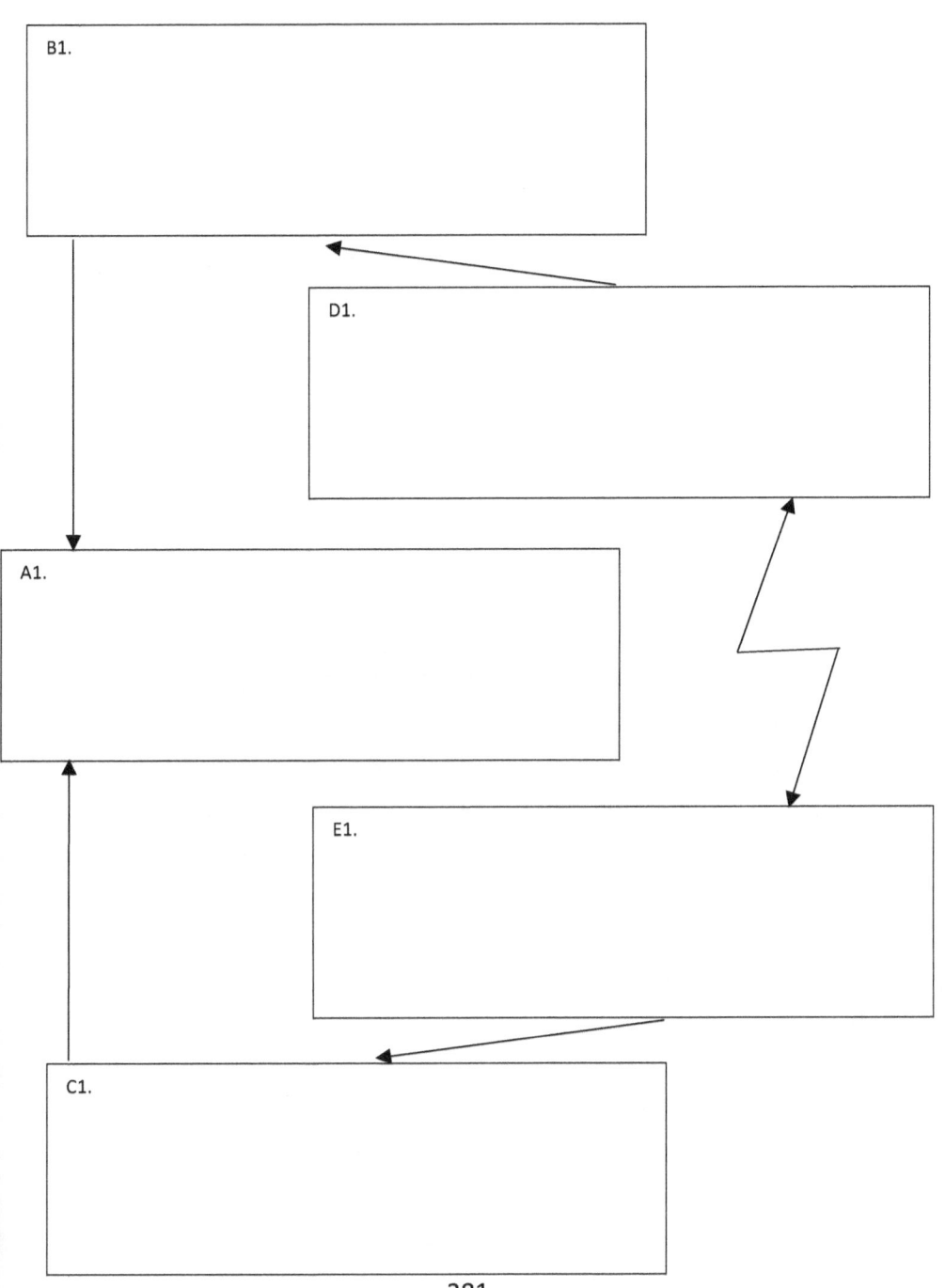

Step 6a:

ABA1

ACA1

BDA1

Silver Bullets

CEA1

BEA1

CDA1

DEA1

Step 3b.

Silver Bullets

Step 4b.

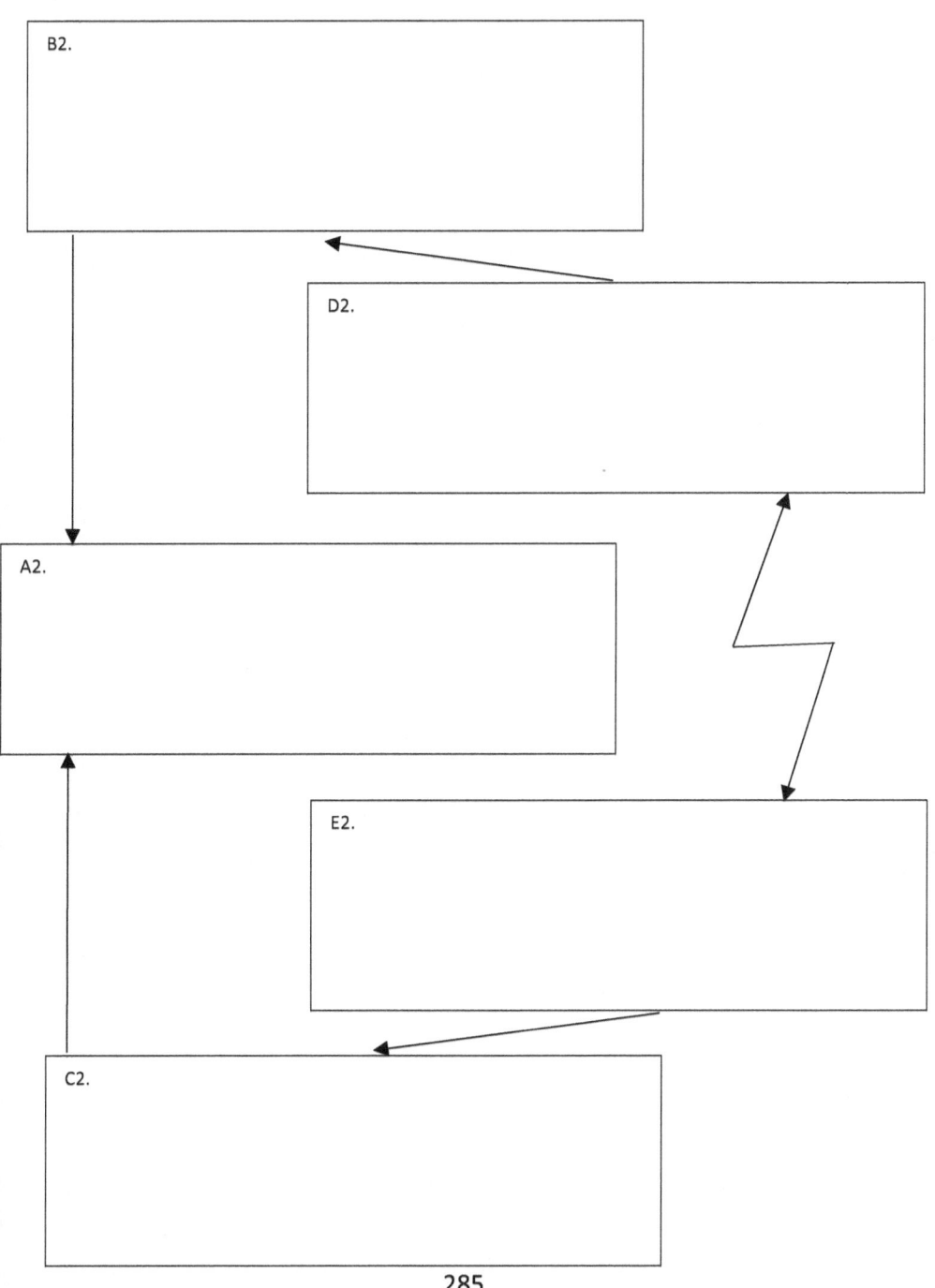

Step 6b:

ABA2

ACA2

BDA2

Silver Bullets

CEA2

BEA2

CDA2

DEA2

Step 3c.

Silver Bullets

Step 4c.

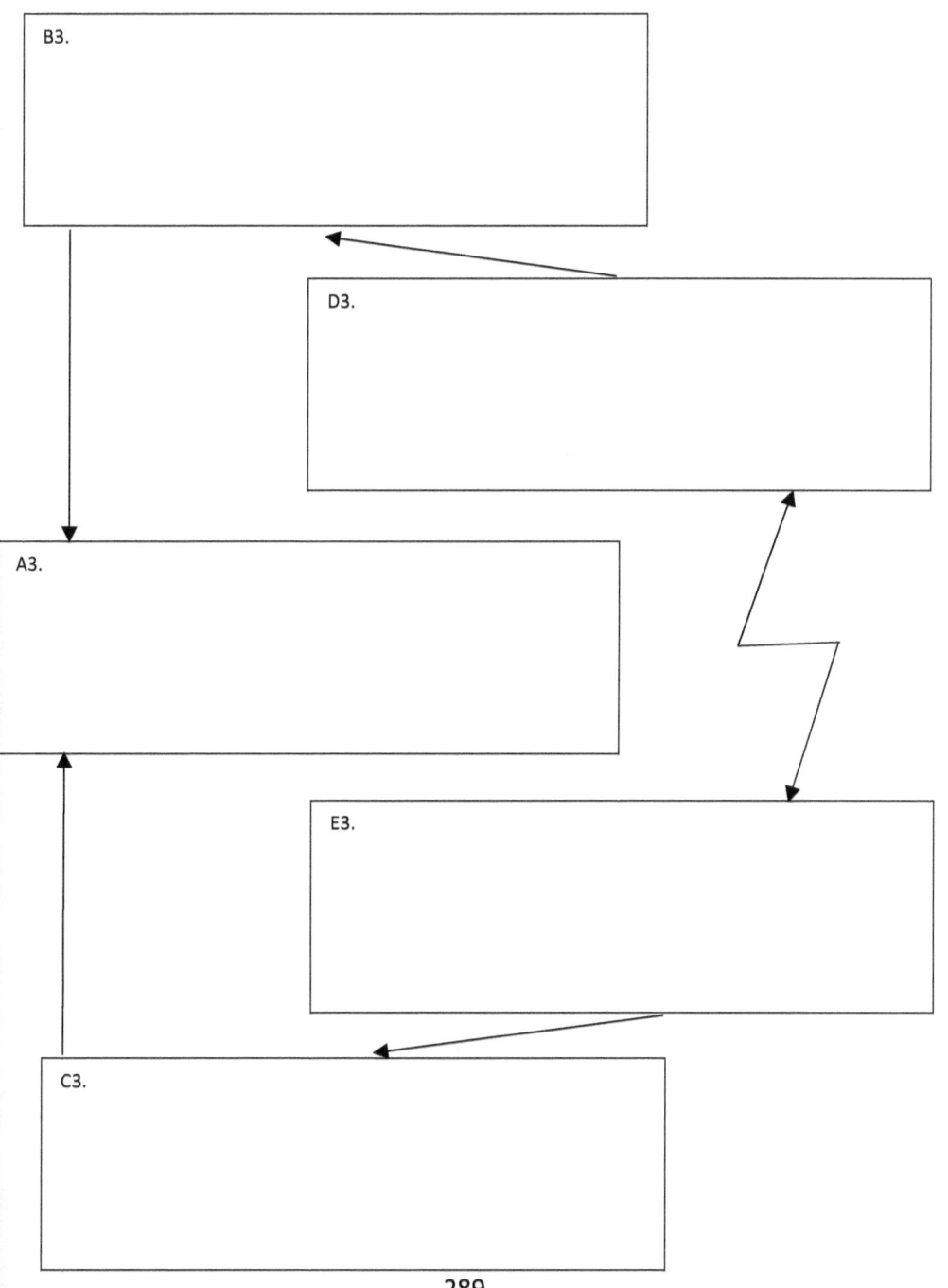

Step 6a:

ABA3

ACA3

BDA3

Silver Bullets

CEA3

BEA3

CDA3

DEA3

Step 7.

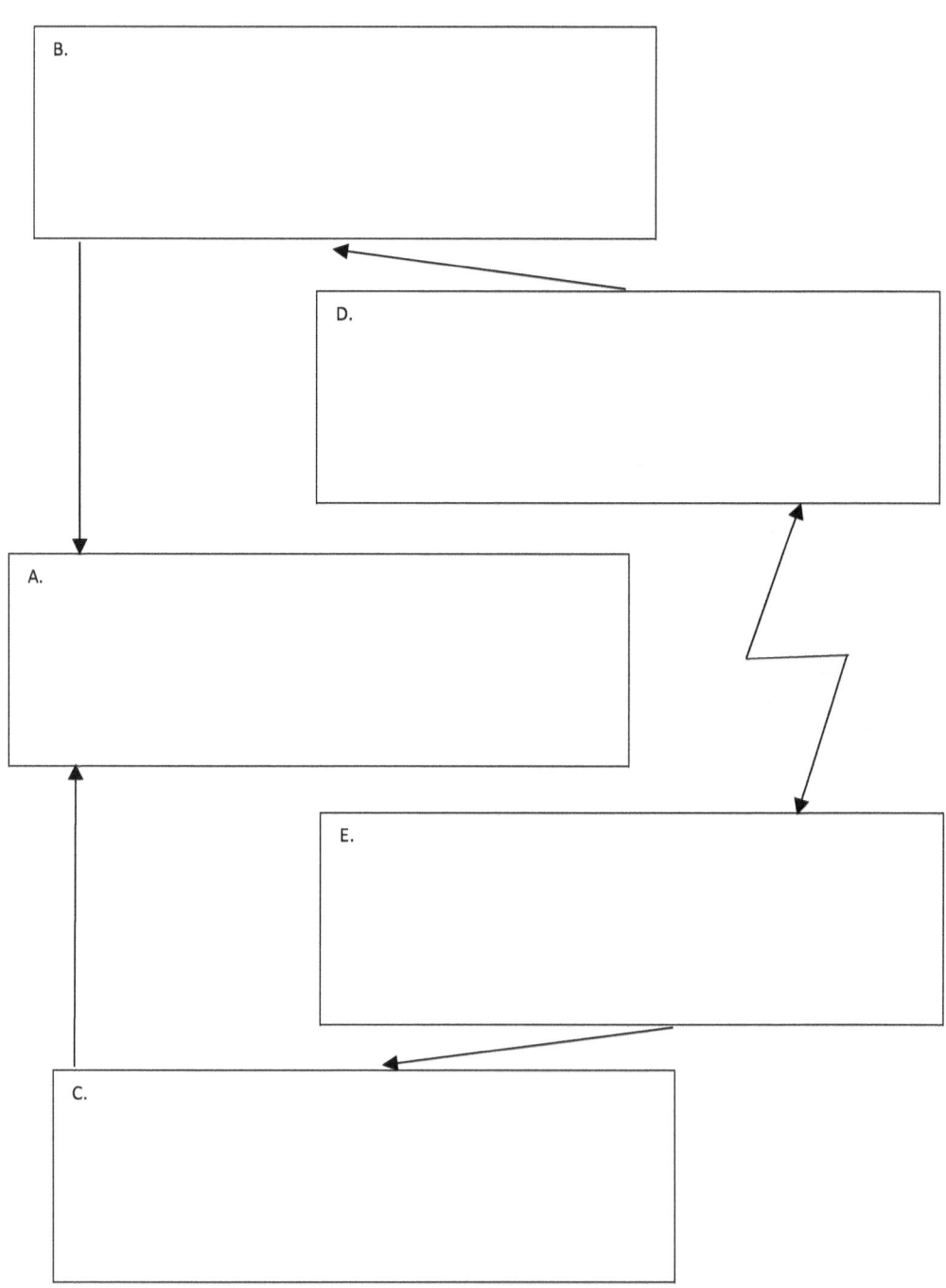

Silver Bullets

Step 8:

Generic ABA

Generic ACA

Generic BDA

Generic CEA

Generic BEA

Generic CDA

Generic DEA

Silver Bullets

Step 9.

Generic ABI

Generic ACI

Generic BDI

Generic CEI

Generic BEI

Generic CDI

Generic DEI

Silver Bullets

Step 10a.

Adapted ABI for UDE 1

Adapted ACI for UDE 1

Adapted BDI for UDE 1

Adapted CEI for UDE 1

Adapted BEI for UDE 1

Adapted CDI for UDE 1

Adapted DEI for UDE 1

Silver Bullets

Step 10a.

Adapted ABI for UDE 2

Adapted ACI for UDE 2

Adapted BDI for UDE 2

Adapted CEI for UDE 2

Adapted BEI for UDE 2

Adapted CDI for UDE 2

Adapted DEI for UDE 2

Silver Bullets

Step 10a.

Adapted ABI for UDE 3

Adapted ACI for UDE 3

Adapted BDI for UDE 3

Adapted CEI for UDE 3

Sources and Additional Reading

Cox, James F., and John G. Schleier. *Theory of Constraints Handbook*. McGraw-Hill, 2010.

Cox, Jeff, et al. *Hanging Fire: Achieving Predictable Results in an Uncertain World, a Business Novel*. AGI/Goldratt Institute, 2014.

Goldratt, E. M., and John L. Cox. *The Goal*. Gower Publishing Company, Limited, 1993.

www.ingramcontent.com/pod-product-compliance
Lightning Source LLC
Chambersburg PA
CBHW031918240526
45464CB00021B/76